QUILTS OF ALASKA

QUILTS OF ALASKA
A Textile Album of the Last Frontier

Rachel Beck
Dana Fobes Bowne
Anne Caston
Peter L. Corey
June E. Hall
Willette Janes
Debbie Manion
Ann Fienup-Riordan
Elizabeth Shapland
Mary Beth Smetzer

Text Editor ❖ Alma Harris
Photographs by Ron Klein
Design by Laura Lucas Design

GASTINEAU CHANNEL HISTORICAL SOCIETY
JUNEAU, ALASKA

This book accompanies the exhibit *Quilts of Alaska: A Textile Album of the Last Frontier*, Alaska State Museum, Juneau, May 13 - September 29, 2001. Guest Curator June E. Hall

Gastineau Channel Historical Society,
PO Box 21264, Juneau, Alaska 99802-1264.

Library of Congress Control Number 00-136488
ISBN # 0-9704815-0-0
First Edition

Notes on abbreviations:
AQS = Alaska Quilt Survey
ASL = Alaska State Library
PCA = Photographic Archive Collection

We are grateful to New Mexico Press for their permission to reprint "How Eskimo Women Spoil Their Cloth" by Ann Fienup-Riordan which appeared in *To Honor and Comfort: Native Quilting Traditions*, 1997.

(cover) "Duck Neck" quilt, Jenny Rasmuson, AQS 690s. (Also see page 58.)

(end papers) CACTUS BASKET detail, 1865-1900, unknown maker, possibly made in Iowa; cotton, pattern pieced, 70" x 82", Collection of Cindy Merriam, AQS 772v.

(half-title page) POPPY detail, AQS 53j. (Also see page 37.)

(opposite title page) DIAMOND IN THE SQUARE variation, 1865-1900, Florence or Abigail Turnbull; cotton, irregular pieced, 83" x 91", Collection of Deborah R. Turnbull, AQS 717k.

(title page) CRAZY detail, AQS 180j. (Also see page 20.)

(left) SPIDERWEB STAR variation, c.1901, Pappy Shissler, Sunbury, Pennsylvannia; cotton, irregular pieced, 12" each, Collection of Sandra Shissler, AQS 940a. These stars are foundation pieced on newspaper and older members of the owner's family were kept occupied with this piecework.

(back cover) HEXAGON pieces, 1865-1900, unknown maker, North Carolina; cotton, pattern pieced, 2" hexagons, Collection of Jenny Stevens, AQS 1369ko. These quilt pieces were found in the attic of the family home built in Elizabeth City, North Carolina in 1898. The paper for the foundation piecing appears to be from bills of lading used in the family wholesale hardware business.

(back cover) Lithographic advertising card for Merrick's thread commemorating the search for the North Pole. Collection of Laura Lucas.

CRAZY detail, 1880-1980, Dolly Chynoweth and descendants, Michigan and Alaska; silk and velvet, irregular pieced, 63" x 66", Collection of Karen. E. Eddy, AQS 1037f. This is one of the many quilts from the survey which was completed by family members many years after it was started — in this case 100 years.

CONTENTS

Acknowledgments 6

Preface 9
June E. Hall

Introduction 12
Rachel Beck

1   Rushing to Alaska 16
Willette Janes

2   Taking Comfort 32
June E. Hall

3   Finding the Time 56
*Dana Fobes Bowne, Anne Caston,
Elizabeth Shapland, and Mary Beth Smetzer*

4   Sharing a Tradition 70
Peter L. Corey and Ann Fienup-Riordan

5   Snakes and Streaks of Lightning 80
Debbie Manion

Appendix 103

AQS Database 104

Endnotes 107

Bibliography 110

Index 111

THE ALASKA QUILT SURVEY and this publication have been a labor of love. The survey began as a local community effort, and with generous support, grew beyond all expectation. We are especially grateful to the individuals and families who willingly shared their quilts and trustingly loaned historic materials. We have received marvelous gifts in the form of time, knowledge and companionship. Our sense of humor, tested from the project's inception to this bright conclusion, remains intact.

Our Discovery Days were made successful by the community coordinators, and by the many volunteers who quickly learned their duties and performed them so cheerfully. We are also grateful to the organizations and institutions that provided the facilities for our Discovery Days. Volunteers and local sponsors are listed by registration site:

ACKNOWLEDGMENTS

Anchorage *Log Cabin Quilters*, formed 1979 ▲ Local Coordinator: Jackie Carley ▲ Jean Campbell, Irene Stewart, Jan Sant, Pat Sims, JoAnn Johnson, Judy Wedemeyer, Sharon Hamlen, Rachel Korshin, Sandee Frederick, Cathy Shultz, Mary Huey, Maggie Plunkett, LaVonne DeBoer, Beth Horton, Diann Sewald, Darlene Appel, Sharon Abbot and staff at the Anchorage Museum of History and Art; Kristine Abshire

Cordova *Cordova Historical Museum and Library* ▲ Local Coordinator: Cathy Sherman ▲ Diane Hawley, Mary Davis, Jennifer Strange, Aleen Brown, Becki Chapek, Diane Rubio

Fairbanks *Cabin Fever Quilters Guild*, formed 1979 ▲ Local Coordinators: Joni Simpson and Barbara Doogan ▲ Martie Lamont, Jennifer Preston, Mary Beth Smetzer, Pamela Gandarellis, Wendy Arundale, Ann-Lillian Schell, Karen Enoch, Ellen Coughenour, Corlis Taylor, Anne Apalsch, Robin Davis, Amy Larson, Lonnie Miller, Laura Fenton, Karyn Janssen, Pat Batemen, Pat Knopf, Mary Worrall, Dana Bowne, Gwen Eicholz, Sara Gislason, Kathy Richardson, Jane Zimmerman, Pam Harris, Nannette Rouleau, Jan Raugust; Hands All Around Fabrics

Haines *Ripinsky Rippers*, formed 1993 ▲ Local Coordinator: Becky Nash ▲ Leslee Downer, Betty DeFranco, Dorothy Sargent, Morinda Stuart

Homer *Pratt Museum* ▲ Local Coordinator: Julia Clymer ▲ Sue Lamb, Molly Custer, Janet Klein, Tirzah Parsons, Bobby Paulino, Arlene Ronda, Melody Chesley, Gail Parsons, Marilyn Schoder, Virginia Marks, Kathleen Cashin

Juneau *Gastineau Channel Historical Society and Capital City Quilters*, formed 1984 ▲ Local Coordinator: Mary Ann Vaughan ▲ Kay Holmes, Chris Reid, Rachel Beck, Debbie Manion, Millie Brazil, Penelope Goforth, Dorothy Frary, Suzanne Hand, Willette Janes, Beth Melville, Elizabeth Cole, Nancy Cooperrider, June E. Hall, Dee Williams, Katherine Shaw, Sue Kilka, Lucille Weir, Kyoko Streuber, Deborah Byrd, Mary Pat Wyatt, Carol Race, Phyllis Davis, Maude Stillwell, Mary Lou King, Willa Allison, Maria Moya, Lonnie Miller, Robin Ross

Kenai and Soldotna *Kenai Peninsula Piecemakers Quilt Group, formed 1984, and Robin Place Fabrics* ▲ Local Coordinators: David and Kathy Wartinbee, Shelia Holtzen, Sue Brown and Pat Reese ▲ Jeneane Benedict, Sue Bowen, Mary Bickel, Janet Cissell, Brenda Cook, Sharon Faucheux, Diane Henwood, Lily Huebsh, Pat Kissee, Chris Lemen, Janie Lewis, LaVon Lockner, Dawn Marcinkowski, Chris Miller, Kathy Sexton, Juli Sexton, Bev Smith, Francesca Stetson, Donna Tomlinson, Rae Vierck, Lucy Volk, Betty West

▲ Other contributors: Peninsula Grace Brethren Church, Trinity Greenhouse, Kenai Fabric Center, Peninsula Clarion, Peninsula Dispatch, Kenai Community Library, Leta Buska, Emily DeForest, Lavonne Currier, Betty Chittenden

Ketchikan *Rainy Day Quilt Guild*, formed 1988 ▲ Local Coordinator: Judy Madden ▲ Judy Eller, Madalyn Palensky, Peggy Gelbrich, Cindy Moore, Susan Bubla, Nancy Kennedy, Dena Conley, Margie Thynes, Debby Turnbull, Barbara Massenburg, Lindley Gifford

Kodiak *Kodiak Bear Claw Quilters*, formed 1990 ▲ Local Coordinators: Rae Jean Blaschke and Vicki Carmichael ▲ Betty Arudt, Jenny Stevens, Gail Kozak, Leah Bush, Sandy Peotter, Ann Stone, Ellen Lester, Tempe Berestof

Nome *Carrie McLain Memorial Museum* staff

Palmer ▲ Local Coordinator: Sara Jansen ▲ Ann Leuenburger, Bea Adler, Patty Rosnel, Eowyn L. Evey, Gerry Keeling, Palmer Historical Society members, Dorothy Page Museum staff, Wasilla

Petersburg *Rain Country Quilters*, formed 1988 ▲ Local Coordinator: Susan Bjorkquist Holmes ▲ Sylvia Nilsen, Sue Flint, Liz Pawuk, Marilyn Menish Meucci, Sheryl Leekley, Cathy Amberson, Betsy Fernau, Pearl Crain, Marjorie G. Colpitts, Cathy Colpitts Cronlund

Seward *Seward Quilt Guild*, formed 1994 ▲ Local Coordinator: Shelia Squires ▲ Donna Glenz, Kirstie Leslie; Resurrection Bay Historical Society

Sitka *Ocean Wave Quilters*, formed 1986 ▲ Local coordinator: Janine Holzman ▲ Brenda Kelley, Tamara Fondell, Carol Music, Galen Paine, Dee West, Marilyn Oen, Heather Baines, Sabra Jenkins, Mary McGraw, Sheryl Ginn, Vienna Vaden, Feryl Woodworth, Alicia Armstead-Harris

Skagway *Skagway Museum* ▲ Local Coordinator: Judy Munns, Director ▲ Su Rappleye, Clydene Sitton, Lynda Skipper, Julene Surdyk, Anna Kirk, Pat Taylor

Valdez *Valdez Museum* ▲ Local Coordinators: Joe Leahy, Director and Trudy Koszarek ▲ Vicky J. Wood, Karen Frye, Jody Morgan, Sheila MacDonald, Phyllis Johnson, Jeanne Kirkland

Wrangell *Friends of the Wrangell Museum* ▲ Local Coordinator: Janell Privet ▲ Kathy Angerman, Lisa Fabrel, Marlene Clarke, Maggie Lampton, Diane O'Brien, Olga Norris, Roberta Floyd, Ken Mason; Wrangell Museum Curator, Teresa Thibault and staff

Additional Support

From the beginning, the survey had unwavering support from the Gastineau Channel Historical Society. Members of the Board of Directors and the Society who have, in their own special way, supported this project through the years are Gary Gillette, Willette Janes, Alma Harris, Nora Toner, Chapin Heumann, Virginia Breeze, Reneé Hughes, Marie Darlin, and Virginia Post.

Special recognition goes to Bruce Kato, Chief Curator at the Alaska State Museum, who has been instrumental in sharing our vision, and to the Museum staff for their support.

Donations

Major donations for the survey and the publication were received over the years from both public and private sources.

Elmer E. Rasmuson of Anchorage made a financial gift which truly made this book possible. Other donations were received from: Alaska State Museum, Friends of the Alaska State Museum, Alaska Humanities Forum, Grace E. Hall, Leighty Foundation, and the Anchorage Log Cabin Quilters.

These donors generously offered to "Sponsor a Page": Rain Country Quilters, Petersburg; Cabin Fever Quilters Guild, Fairbanks; Judy Hopkins, In Honor of Lois Dafoe and Ruth Strickling; Alma and Don Harris, In Honor of Betty N. Earl; Rachel Beck, In Honor of D. Gail Beck and Della Oonk; Capital City Quilters, Juneau; Kodiak Bear Paw Quilters Guild, Kodiak; Kay Holmes, In Honor of my fellow Steering Committee members; June E. Hall, In Honor of Grace Elizabeth Hall; and Michelle Storer.

Dedicated donations for the publication came from: Madalyn Palensky, In Memory of Stella Holecek Palensky, Elizabeth C. Cole, In Memory of Blanche Shanahan and Annie Castle; Betty Lappi, Marie Darlin, Margie Blankenship, In Honor of Lillie M. Darlin; and Debbie Manion, In Honor of Kathleen Slabodnik.

Publication donors: Ocean Wave Quilters, Sitka; Wendy Arundale, Budd and Paulette Simpson, Anni Stokes and Kim Hutchinson, Paul Emerson, Jean D. Lear, Paul and Gail Beck, Willette Janes, Virginia Post, Ripinski Rippers, Haines.

Other contributors provided waivers, monetary and in-kind donations: Juneau Arts and Humanities Council, Westmark Hotels, Alaska Marine Highway, Mary Pat Wyatt, Curator of the Juneau-Douglas City Museum; Terri Cosper, Museum Loan Network, Michigan State University Museum, New Mexico Press, Royal British Columbia Museum, *The Daily Oklahoman*, Phyllis Davis, Brad Curé, and Marcia Nye.

Technical Assistance

Technical assistance and encouragement came from many directions.

We were fortunate to have Barbara Brackman and Judy Hopkins as knowledgable and inspirational consultants for the project. Art Sutch and Paul Helmar advised us on photographic needs for the early Discovery Days, and John Ingalls designed equipment. Art Peterson and Maria Moya aided with grant requirements. Sharp-eyed proofing and accuracy in editing the publication came from Virginia Breeze, Judy Hopkins, Merikay Waldvogel, and Odette Foster. Precision digital imaging was done by Eric Torgerson.

Laura Lucas, with her exceptional design skills and creative insights, contributed far more than just graphic layouts.

Alma Harris, with her extraordinary patience and sensitivity, edited the manuscript from some rough beginnings to final form.

The survey database was developed with the patient help of Joyce Sarles; data was diligently entered by Ashley Badger, Michael M. Partlow, Jim Disdier, and Michael McGee.

Our book photographer, Ron Klein, captured the unique quality of each quilt and allowed us to showcase them as the works of art they truly are. He was aided by Judy Regan, Michelle Storer, Johanna Smith, Terri Hoskinson, Glenn Hoskinson, Wendy Swedell, Sadie Ingalls, Toni Shattenburg, Jill McAllister, Willette Janes, and Claire Ishii.

Research Assistance

Our research was aided by individuals and organizations who shared their time, knowledge and expertise: Robert DeArmond, American Quilt Study Group, Anchorage Museum of History and Art, Mary Ann Slemmons, Kathy Wartinbee, Merikay Waldvogel, University of Alaska Archives, Alaska State Historical Library staff, Marsha MacDowell, Steve Thomas, Bureau of Indian Affairs; Alaska State Archives; Bruce Parham, Federal Archives-Pacific Alaska Region; Connie Munro, Jean Hall, Jane Haigh, Bob Burke, Dan Hopson, Gerry Keeling, Smithsonian National Museum of American History staff; Lydia Black, Luba C. Blinova, Dr. Irina N. Ukhanova, Candy Waugaman, the Abby Aldrich Rockefeller Folk Art Museum, and Mary Bywater Cross.

We apologize for any names inadvertently omitted and accept the responsibility for unintended inaccuracies. We are grateful to each and every person who made this project possible.

THE HOUSE JACK BUILT detail, 1925-1950, Selma (Cross) Voris, Flippin, Kentucky; cotton, pattern pieced, 64" x 78", Collection of Rebecca J. Voris, AQS 907a. The fabric in this quilt includes bright feed sack material. (Detail on opposite page.)

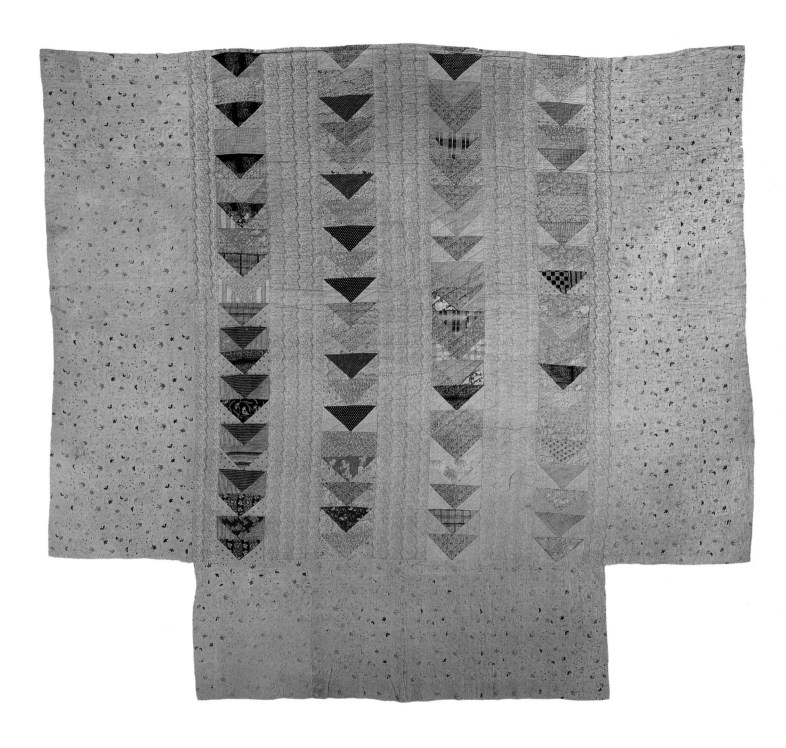

WILD GOOSE CHASE, 1800-1840, unknown maker, probably made in New England; cotton and linen, pattern pieced, 100" x 104", Collection of Oliver Backlund, AQS 1052f. A wonderful mixture of roller printed, calico and homespun fabrics make up this quilt.

ROCKY ROAD TO
KANSAS variation
detail, 1925-1959,
unnamed maker,
Quincy, California; wool,
cotton and synthetics,
pattern and irregular
pieced, 77" x 92",
Collection of Janie Lewis,
AQS 1185ke. After the
maker's husband died,
she made several quilts
using black fabric.

PREFACE
June E. Hall

QUILTS OF ALASKA: A Textile Album of the Last Frontier, the exhibit and this book, comes exactly thirty years after the ground breaking quilt show organized by Jonathan Holstein and Gail van der Hoof in 1971. *Abstract Design in American Quilts,* their exhibit at the Whitney Museum, helped fuel the current quiltmaking revival. The visual power of these quilts astonished both the museum staff and the viewing public. In the new context of a prestigious New York art museum, quilts were finally elevated to a higher status in the traditional, though arbitrary, hierarchy of art objects. Because context strongly defines any object and limits how it is seen, the removal of quilts from their traditonal setting to this gallery clearly aided in convincing the public that quilts were after all, "art." Until this time, quilts generally had been considered a folk handicraft which may have been a blessing in disguise. Women quiltmakers in America, long neglected by the official art world, developed their own vocabulary of color and designs. Left free to work independently of "fine art" criteria, these American quiltmakers experimented and invented with the formal elements of abstract design. In the process of crafting quilts, a private expressive world of their own making was created where they could be their own best judges and worst critics. Quiltmakers had made, whether consciously or intuitively, the same aesthetic choices as Matisse or Mary Cassatt.

In the intervening years numerous exhibits have solidly established quilts as more than naïve folk art. One of the purposes of the

Alaska quilt exhibit and this book is to help reclaim the domestic framework as a rightful place for making art and to emphasize the importance of the women's art made in that setting. Unlike the Whitney exhibit, we have chosen to go beyond aesthetic judgment and whenever possible include the history of the quilts, the connection between these quilted objects and their creative origin, and the story of the makers. The quilts we have chosen to present are not just the spectacular ones, but those that have meaning beyond their aesthetic appeal — those which served to illustrate the many personal and cultural purposes of quilts. Our exhibit and book are about this special group of art objects and the significance of the Alaska Quilt Survey documentation process.

The Alaska Quilt Survey came toward the end of the enormous grass roots effort of documenting American quilts; our survey was patterned after other projects completed over many years. When we decided to record the quilts in Alaska, we had no idea the project would become much more than just a gathering of facts and a counting of threads. We did not realize how the process would affect us, nor how important it was to the people who took part. The very nature of quilts brought out the intimate relationship of art objects to their owners or makers. Throughout the survey years, questions became answers, and answers became questions. Would anyone come to our Discovery Days? Why did so many people come? What kind of quilts would be brought in? Would there be any early "Alaskan style" quilts? Why did this style begin to appear only in the 1970s? Why would someone proudly bring in a family quilt that had been so used it was barely recognizable? Why did people come for awhile and then stay all day? Why did we feel so humbled and yet exuberant at the end of an exhausting day? We really hadn't thought at all about what Discovery Days *really* were. Gradually we realized that this project was much more than an academic documentation, and the honor in taking part was not ours alone. Our Discovery Days had created their own unique context and an unexpected opportunity for recognition and understanding.

What we thought would be a rather methodical process evolved into a dynamic interchange between visual objects, the spoken word, and the participants. The strong visual and tactile quality of the quilts, and their significance in people's lives, often evoked unexpected impassioned responses. We had not suspected that the quilts would hold such tightly wrapped family histories — stories so compelling that words were not enough to explain their true meanings. Our careful planning had not prepared us to be witnesses to startling changes in family relationships when discovered for the first time. We could only stand quietly by when the sorrow for a loved one long gone was revealed by a hand softly passing over the top of a quilt. Tiny stitches and straight seams helped build a self-confidence in those left behind. Around the dating tables, families remembered together what they should not forget. Discovery Days were easily transformed into spontaneous overtures of oral and visual delight.

HEXAGON detail, 1840-1865, unknown maker; cotton, pattern pieced, 71" x 76", Collection of Sheila and Earl Holtzen, AQS 1228ke. This unusual variation of the Hexagon pattern was believed to have been made during the Civil War. It is entirely hand-pieced and quilted.

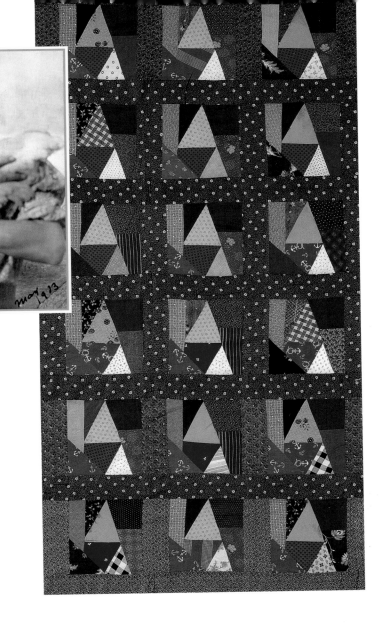

(right) Bertha Laura (Grossardt) Sparling in May, 1913.

(far right) Unknown pattern top detail, 1900-1925, Bertha Laura (Grossardt) Sparling, possibly made in Kansas; cotton, pattern pieced, 80" x 81", Collection of Jane Zerbe, AQS 1115f. "My dad let me select [this top] from those in his mom's wooden chest. There were 8-10 in the box. She made them while single."

A Discovery Day was really a reciprocal event, not unlike other ceremonies based on sharing of materials or objects within a community. Other events in Alaska, including the Northwest Coast Native potlatch and the Nelson Island Eskimo seal party covered in Chapter Four, create a similar presentation setting for objects considered significant to an individual or group. As part of these activities, meaningful objects are offered for recognition and initiate the process of binding people together through time and space. Most of the quilts presented at Discovery Days had never been publicly viewed, and the Discovery Day process was unfamiliar to a majority of the participants. In this setting, quilts served one of the traditional roles of art — to receive and become the bearer of personal and group history and identity. The words spoken and stories told about the objects and their owners or makers added depth to their meaning. The observer and object completed each other. The outstanding quilts, when raised to be photographed, were universally recognized and appreciated. Volunteers treated all quilts with respect and acknowledged their importance. Participants left with new regard for their quilts. Some realized for the first time they were keepers of a heritage in cloth.

The documentation process helped everyone involved better understand the immensely important functions that quilts serve in people's lives, especially for women. After we viewed many hundreds of quilts, it was clear that most makers had made formal aesthetic choices. But just as important was the quilts' function to preserve family and personal history and identity. Quilts, though serving a practical purpose, have their real significance in more intangible and harder to define spheres, often rising from domestic dramas that molded the maker and family. Invested in even the simplest quilt was an expression of everyday experience translated into visual poetry.

June Hall
Alaska Quilt Survey
May 2000

CRAZY QUILT, dated 1888, unknown maker, possibly made in New York State; silk, satin and velvet, irregular pieced, 39" x 80", Collection of Wendy Arundale, AQS 1331f. "This quilt belonged to my paternal grandmother, Mary Stewart "Matie" (Gage) Hanford. Throughout much of her adult life it lay folded on the back of her Victorian mohair sofa and I never saw it used for anything but decoration."

INTRODUCTION
Rachel Beck

FOR SEVEN YEARS, the Alaska Quilt Survey searched for quilts in a vast land that unfolds more like a country than a state. Its perimeter unravels with 33,904 miles of saltwater coastline around an area equivalent to Washington, Oregon, California, Arizona, and Nevada. A place of extremes, time flows between endless days of summer light and endless nights of winter darkness. The landscape ranges from the dense, green, temperate rainforests in the Southeast Panhandle to the dry, treeless tundra of the Arctic slopes. In our quest for Alaskan quilts, we rode ferries past glaciers into small Southeast towns nestled along the coast and flew past Mount McKinley, the highest peak in North America. Anchorage is home to almost half of Alaska's 621,400 residents, while the rest of the population lives in smaller cities, or "bush" villages. However, Alaska's vastness is countered by the closeness of its inhabitants. Rewards of our search included meeting hundreds of generous and thoughtful people who shared their time and treasures during the seventeen statewide Discovery Days. This is the story of that search and the quilts we found.

The impetus for the Alaskan quilt project was an early 1980s article by Barbara Brackman. This noted quilt historian recounted the quilt documentation projects taking place in the United States. Adding Alaska to the map of quilt history seemed important. Under the sponsorship of the Gastineau Channel Historical Society in Juneau, interested women made and raffled a local history quilt in 1990. A year later, with these funds, the historical society held a quilt dating workshop led by Brackman.

After learning about the "clues in the calico," the Alaska Quilt Survey was formed by a steering committee including Rachel Beck, Kay Holmes, June Hall, Debbie Manion, Carol Thilenius, and Mary Ann Vaughan. We held our first Discovery Day at a Juneau mall in 1992 with the help of the Capital City Quilters. We were thrilled to have 76 quilts to register; the response was so enthusiastic, a second event was scheduled.

In 1994 Sitka's Ocean Wave Quilters voiced interest in documenting their community's quilts, and in January two steering committee members traveled to Sitka for a Discovery Day. Although Sitka lies only 95 miles southwest of Juneau, both communities are inaccessible by road, the travel choices were limited to a forty-minute airplane flight or a nine-hour ferry ride. The only realistic option was to fly. For each Discovery Day, steering committee members faced similar logistical decisions. During quilt Discovery Days at Juneau and Sitka, more than 380 quilts were registered.

Interest in Discovery Days gained momentum from places as far away as Fairbanks. We then realized that greater resources were needed to reach these distant communities and that our scope needed to become statewide. The Alaska Quilt Survey evolved quickly. We applied for and received a large Alaska Humanities Forum grant; additional funding from the Alaska State Museum and the Friends of the Alaska State Museum made it possible to conduct Discovery Days in fifteen communities.

We outlined our goals for the survey: to document the historical, geographical and social connections between quilts and their Alaskan context; to bring quilts as material art and artifact into the wider community consciousness; to record the voices of Alaskan women telling their own stories of family heirlooms; to reveal any cross-cultural influences in quilt design and production; to heighten the appreciation of quilts and textiles as art forms; to promote the conservation and preservation of quilts; to convey the passion of quilting in women's lives and to emphasize the domestic context in which much of women's art is made. In the survey, although we did register contemporary quilts, we chose to emphasize quilts made before 1959, the year of Alaskan statehood.

From 1994 to 1998 we journeyed to the southeast communities of Sitka, Haines, Skagway, Petersburg, Wrangell, and Ketchikan and to the northern towns of Valdez, Cordova, Kenai, Soldotna, Homer, Seward, Kodiak, and Palmer — traveling twice to Anchorage and Fairbanks. Although we were unable to go to Nome, the helpful staff of the Carrie McLain Museum assisted in uncovering two significant local quilts. At every Discovery Day, volunteers provided innumerable hours of enthusiastic labor to process approximately 1,530 quilts. They also supplied potluck lunches, warm dinners, and often a cozy place to sleep. The requested visit to a local fabric store was always accommodated.

We scheduled our trips for the winter months, as summer is a time when many Alaskans earn their seasonal wages. Winter

This small advertising card was used for the Juneau 1990 quilt raffle which raised initial funds for the project. The quilt was won locally and later purchased by the Juneau-Douglas City Museum. Collection of the Alaska Quilt Survey.

(left) The first Discovery Day held in 1992 in Juneau shows volunteers (from left to right) Lonnie Miller, Allan Collais (quilt owner), Mary Ann Vaughan, Debbie Manion and Kay Holmes examining Allan's family quilt squares which had been carried twice over the Oregon Trail and survived a trunk trip down the flooded Mississippi River. AQS photograph by June E. Hall.

Denali (Mt. McKinley) from Wonder Lake, Denali National Park and Preserve, Alaska. Photo by Ron Klein.

travel in Alaska is a challenge at best, and one trip had us wondering if we would ever arrive home. We were diverted to Sitka because Juneau's weather was under the minimum for landing due to fog. The small Sitka airport was jammed with hundreds of stranded passengers, including the newly crowned state basketball champions and their excited entourage. We decided to fly to Anchorage, a thousand miles away, to increase our chances of finding an open flight back to Juneau the next day. We prevailed on a friend for floor space that night, and luckily made the flight home in the morning. Exciting side trips on a smaller scale abounded, like the cabin-stay in Homer that required standing on the back of a dog sled and being towed by snowmobile over more than half a mile of hummocks and dark trails. On another Southeast flight above white capped waves into Skagway, our four-seat plane bounced around in the turbulence, and a committee member hit her head on the cabin ceiling. She looked down to observe that her seat was not bolted securely. We were always grateful to reach any destination.

After the formulation of a database and assessment of the registered quilts, criteria for the book and show selection were developed.

The criteria emphasized construction and design; Alaskan historical context; significant or interesting family history; quilts as cultural or cross-cultural documents; and quilts as an individual, expressive medium. The steering committee spent countless, agonizing hours making selections and chose not to showcase only the "best of." In the final selection of quilts for the exhibit and book, we selected primarily quilts made before 1959. Many wonderful contemporary Alaskan quilts were registered and many more have yet to be uncovered; they are deserving of their own book.

Through freezing temperatures, bumpy rides, and thousands of miles we met warm-hearted, caring people and found textile treasures. From a pristine contest-winning quilt to a much loved but threadbare Crazy quilt to a rare "Duck Neck" quilt, we found the uniqueness and diversity that this "great land" embodies. In this land of extremes, we discovered great wealth.

Rachel Beck
Alaska Quilt Survey
May 2000

ALASKA

○ locations where quilts were registered by the Alaska Quilt Survey

0   100   200
MILES

Laura Lucas Design

Arctic Ocean

BROOKS RANGE

Arctic Circle

Point Barrow

Kivalina ●

○ **Nome**

Bering Sea

Yukon River

Yukon River

Mt. McKinley ▲

UNITED STATES

CANADA

YUKON TERRITORY

Dawson City ●

Yukon River

● **Fairbanks**

ALASKA RANGE

○ **Palmer**
○ **Anchorage**
○ **Valdez**
Kenai ○ ○
○ **Soldotna**   ○ **Cordova**
Homer ○   ○ **Seward**
○ **Seldovia**

BRITISH COLUMBIA

Chilkoot Pass

Yakutat ●

Pribilof Is ○

Aleutian Islands

○ **Kodiak**

Gulf of Alaska

PACIFIC OCEAN

Haines ○ ○ **Skagway**
○ **Juneau**
Petersburg
Sitka ○
Wrangell ○
Ketchikan ○

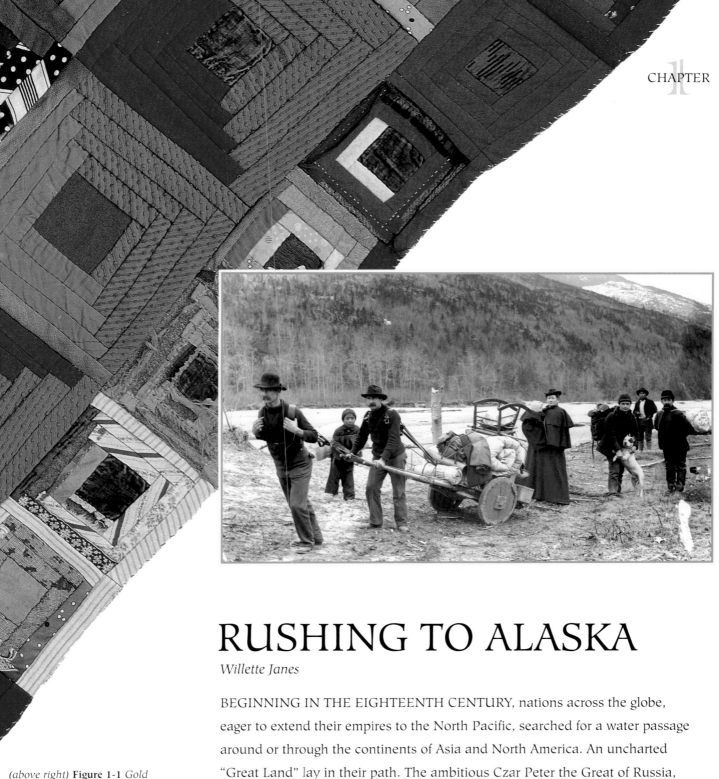

(above right) **Figure 1-1** *Gold seekers off to the Klondike often found it hard to leave every comfort of home behind. Winter and Pond photographers, ASL PCA 87.664.*

(left) **Figure 1-2** *LOG CABIN top detail, 1865-1900, Helena Smith Sharp, possibly made in Missouri; cotton, wool, silk, pattern pieced, 63" x 76", Collection of Courtney Linkous, AQS 1035f. (Also see p. 26.)*

RUSHING TO ALASKA

Willette Janes

BEGINNING IN THE EIGHTEENTH CENTURY, nations across the globe, eager to extend their empires to the North Pacific, searched for a water passage around or through the continents of Asia and North America. An uncharted "Great Land" lay in their path. The ambitious Czar Peter the Great of Russia, who sought opportunity in the North Pacific, commissioned the Danish sea captain Vitus Bering to determine if Russia and North America were one continent. On Bering's second trip in 1741, he made landfall and officially "discovered" Alaska. After Bering's voyages of exploration, the first of the "rushes," a fur rush, began for the valuable sea otter pelts.[1] The search for the first quilts in Alaska was an exploration of a different kind. The stories

SITKA.
VIEW OF THE TOWN FROM THE SOUTH-WEST, MOUNT EDGECOMB BEARING EAST.

Figure 1-3 *Watercolor, Lt. Schreinben (attr.), Sitka. View of the town from the South-west. c.1860. To the left along the beach, the small houses of the Native village are fenced off from the rest of the town. At the center is the spire of Saint Michael's Cathedral of the Russian Orthodox faith, dedicated in 1844. The Governor's House is on the hill high above the harbor. Sitka was founded by Alexandr Baranov in 1804 becoming the largest town in Alaska and center of the trading industry for the Pacific. The artist is thought to have been a Russian naval officer. Alaska State Museum VA.50.*

preserved in these quilts are indeed intertwined with the history of the "Last Frontier." The women who ventured to Alaska seldom wrote about themselves. However, some of the women left behind their own kind of heritage — that of their handiwork — in the loving and creative stitching of quilts.

A Heritage in Handiwork

Because quiltmaking is primarily a woman's craft, searching for the earliest possible quilts led to researching the earliest women in Alaska. European women accompanied some of the first explorers and colonists to Russian America, and those women may have introduced quilt-making. The Russian quilt tradition dates from at least the nineteenth century and probably goes back much earlier;[2] however, no direct references have been found that Russian bed quilts were brought to or made in Alaska during the Russian occupation. Lady Margaretha Etholen, a native of Finland and wife of the sixth governor, Arvid Etholen, who also was Finnish, resided in Sitka from 1840 to 1845.[3] She started a school for creole girls,[4] teaching them needlework, embroidery, languages (French, German, Russian, and English), geography, history, and household arts.[5]

It was not for the want of material that quilts are not found from this period. During the nineteenth century, the Russian colonies had a good supply of fabric. In the shipping records kept by the Russians from 1817 to 1832, various fabrics are listed, some in great quantities. Bombazine, Bengal cotton, seersucker, taffeta, blue Canton cotton, English woolens, frieze, and velveteen plus 1,000 needles were listed as shipments for sale to the colonists or as trade goods.[6] After the transfer of Alaska to the United States in 1867, the Russians began emptying their Sitka warehouses and shipping most of the contents to San Francisco.

According to Robert N. DeArmond "...the warehouses of the Russian-American Company were not only crowded but positively crammed to capacity with an incredible inventory of merchandise, trade goods, materials of nearly every kind imaginable. The Russian colony was reported to have been short of foodstuffs from time to time, but at the end there was no shortage of dry goods, hardware and notions." Among the dry goods were listed 22,000 yards of cloth.[7]

The Russian American-Company administered the Russian colony, and as Lyman

Woodman observed, when the organization went out of business, "The Russians and Creoles who had been, in effect, wards of the company for years were at loose ends...." Not only did the Russians' and Creoles' world fade away,[8] but "During the...summer, before the transfer, boatloads of adventurers, politicians, office-seekers, and aspirants for profit had arrived in Sitka from Seattle, Portland, and San Francisco. A 'motley lot,' as one writer put it. Hoping to make a gain with the new land, they extended the townsite, staking out lots and building shanties for which they charged high prices to newcomers. The Governor's house was pre-empted, 'and some godless individual even recorded a claim for the church.'"[9] Once the transfer was accomplished, "Sitka had some adjusting to do. It had been transformed in a day from a company town, with essentials furnished to a virtual family of employees constituting almost the entire population, to a frontier community under new management with poorly understood rules."[10]

Fortune-seekers

Some of these men and women who rushed excitedly to Alaska for economic opportunity and to make use of the abundant natural resources[11] were counted in the United States Army's 1870 census of the population of Sitka. The total number, 391, did not include the more than 100 soldiers, their wives and families, nor the Native population which was twice that of the foreigners. Of the white inhabitants, around 127 were women over eighteen who labored as prostitutes, laundresses, seamstresses and as midwife, nurse, teacher, toymaker, and snuff maker. At this time, 83 children lived in Sitka.[12] Women, very much a contributing part of the settlement of Alaska in those early years, continued to work at all their traditional occupations, including sewing.

Life on the "Last Frontier," as on any other frontier, made ultimate demands on time, energy, and resourcefulness. Pioneering Alaskan women made sacrifices and contributions

similar to the women of American colonial times when the success of a community hinged on their hard work and fortitude. Frontier women had to "wrest their art from a workday that gave them no relief from life-sustaining chores, no leisure for reflection....They were part of a culture... [that] failed to appreciate the technical complexity and visual sophistication of their work. Yet, with all of this against them, they persevered. These women had the cleverness and insight to realize that their domestic and creative responsibilities could be combined...."[13]

"Worthy of a Czarevitch"

The earliest reference found to a quilt in Alaska appears in the diary of an American, Elizabeth "Libby" (Debois) Beaman. Libby and her husband, John, arrived at the Pribilof Islands in the Bering Sea in 1879. She was the first white woman to stay on the isolated islands of St. Paul and St. George. John was appointed assistant to the U.S special agent who supervised the taking of fur seal pelts.[14] Upon their arrival at St. Paul, Libby was dismayed to discover that they had to share

Figure 1-4 *1894 Inventory ledger of the Alaska Treadwell Gold Mining Company store. Treadwell was a company town and miners and their families could get almost anything they needed at the store, including many fabrics. Courtesy of Richard Wood.*

Figure 1-5 *CRAZY, dated and inscribed in ink, "June 5ᵗʰ, 1888, Hon. Lafayette Dawson From the Ladies of Alaska, Sitka, Alaska," silk, satin and velvet, irregular pieced, 72" x 72", Collection of the Alaska State Museum, Juneau, III.0.979, AQS 180j.*

living space with the senior agent. She resolutely wrote, "It's up to me to make the best of everything and to do so with good grace. We will never survive the two years and keep our sanity unless I do."[15] Libby unpacked their "hampers" and among the items were a large eiderdown that she had quilted for her hope chest and a silk Crazy quilt that she had made with her sister Carrie.[16]

Even though the winters were severe and the killing of seals and the smells of death were repugnant to her, she grew to love the people and the islands' remoteness and stark beauty. However, when Libby became pregnant, the Beamans decided to leave the Pribilof Islands. On the day of their departure in the fall of 1880, an Aleut girl presented Libby with a baby blanket which "she had stitched so carefully — of alternative diamond-shaped patches of pure white and dark belly fur from seal pups. Around it she had sown [sic] a wide border of the rare white fur, truly a beautiful gift and worthy of a czarevitch."[17]

Frequently, quiltmaking has been transferred to other parts of the world through the efforts of missionaries. The same process occurred in Alaska as numerous American and European missionaries arrived. One of the early Presbyterian missionaries who made a reference to quilts in Alaska was Mrs. Eugene (Caroline) Willard who observed that quilts were impractical in the damp rainforest conditions of the Southeast Panhandle. After two years at the Haines Mission, Mrs. Willard noted in an 1883 letter, "blankets (colored ones) were better than quilts, and more easily kept clean than comforts."[18]

Signatures of an Era

Not long after Mrs. Willard commented on the impracticality of quilts, an elegantly embroidered commemorative Crazy *(fig. 1.5)* was made in Sitka. The U. S. Congress finally provided the District of Alaska with a court system and a governor in Sitka. Government officials, support personnel, and their families in this remote center practiced a version of the decorous social life based on Victorian sensibilities. The quilt was given to Judge Lafayette Dawson when he left Sitka in 1888. Dawson had been appointed District Judge for Alaska by President Cleveland[19] and he gained the respect of the people of Sitka through his fair decisions.[20] Because of the forced absence from his wife and for political reasons, he later resigned.[21]

Originally, twenty-one ladies were listed in the Alaska State Museum records as having signed or initialed the blocks of the quilt given to Judge Dawson. The museum's list compared to the actual quilt indicates that some of the names are no longer visible. The majority of the ladies who signed the quilt were teachers and long-time friends. Over the years, some taught the "domestic arts" at the Sitka Industrial Training School, part of the Presbyterian mission. Many of the activities of the missionary teachers who signed the quilt were chronicled in the *North Star*, the mission newsletter, edited by Sheldon Jackson and William Kelly.

(above) **Figure 1-7a**
CRAZY Sitka Rose detail, AQS 180j, dated June 5th, 1888, and inscribed "Hon. Lafayette Dawson, From the Ladies of Alaska." (Also see p. 20.)

(pages 22-23)
Figures 1-7 b-e
CRAZY details, AQS 180j.

In 1880, Reverend and Mrs. Alonzo (Isabella) E. Austin opened the first Native boarding school at the mission. Misses Jennie Pakle and Margaret Powell followed in 1886. Jennie later married B.M. Behrends, a highly successful merchant and banker in Juneau.

A teacher who added her signature was lauded in an 1888 *North Star* issue. "On the arrival of each steamer, throngs of tourists visit the Industrial School at Sitka. One of the departments that never fails to impress and delight them is the Girls' Sewing Room under the efficient management of Mrs. S. S. Winans. The progress made under her instruction is something that needs to be seen to be appreciated. Let some thrifty mother who thinks her three or four boys make much mending, try to picture the scores of rents and hundreds of holes that must pile into the Mission sewing room each week from over 100 boys and 60 romping girls." Mrs. Winans somehow found time to also teach free hand and perspective drawing.[22]

Additional women whose names also appear on the quilt were Mrs. Charles (Josie) Overend, Miss Rhoda Lee, and Elizabeth J. Brady — E. J. B. on the quilt. Elizabeth arrived aboard the steamer *Idaho* and, unlike the others, taught in the public school near the Native village. She later married John G. Brady who became governor of Alaska. Mrs. Whitaker (Alice) M. Grant's husband served as district attorney. M. F. (Mary) Haydon was the vivacious wife of Henry E. Haydon, clerk of the court under Judge Dawson,[23] and she contributed significantly to her community. In December of 1890, "Mrs. H. E. Haydon, of Sitka, desires through the columns of the *Record* to extend her thanks to the people of Juneau who were attending court for their liberality in taking chances in a quilt made by her and raffled for the benefit of Mrs. Daicker, widow of the late Charles Daicker."[24]

In addition to providing asssistance to others, Mrs. Haydon taught embroidery every Tuesday at the Industrial School. The sewing supplies for her class were more plentiful than might be imagined. One ship into Sitka brought stamped patterns for scarfs, table mats and cushions, ribbons, remnants of brocaded silks, satins, velvets, worsteds, and gold morris cloth. This was enough to "set the older girls of the Sitka Mission wild with delight. They had never seen such elegant things before. They had not even imagined that anything half so beautiful existed. It was to them a vision from Fairyland."[25] In 1895, a *North Star* representative visited the sewing room and remarked that the girls were intent upon their work whether working by hand or machine. "These little girls mend, darn, sew quilt pieces and knit."[26]

Women who were not teachers also signed or initialed the Dawson commemorative quilt. Among those was Mrs. Louis L. Williams whose husband was appointed U. S. Marshall in 1890. Arthur K. Delaney was Collector of the Customs, and either his wife or daughter signed her last name on the quilt. The initials L. B. V. probably stood for Lena Vanderbilt, who later married Edward DeGroff, a well-known merchant. R. M. B. is for Mrs. R. M. Baker. [27]

Natalia (Kashevaroff) Kostrometinoff's ink signature on the quilt was found only by the use of a black light. Andrew Kashevaroff, a brother to Natalia, was renowned as the first director of what became the Alaska State Museum and Historical Library and as a priest of St. Nicholas Orthodox Church in Juneau. Natalia, who was of Aleut and Russian descent, married George (Sergius) Kostrometinoff, who was born in Sitka. George served as the long time warden of St. Michael's Cathedral in Sitka and as a linguist. Robert N. DeArmond says of Kostrometinoff, "In this capacity he was so valuable to the American authorities that it was sometimes said that the odd $200,000 in the Alaska purchase price was for the purpose of acquiring George Kostrometinoff." [28]

Figure 1-8 *George and Natalia (Kashevaroff) Kostrometinoff, c.1895. Natalia's ink signature on the Dawson Crazy quilt was barely visible after 100 years. ASL PCA 01.118a.*

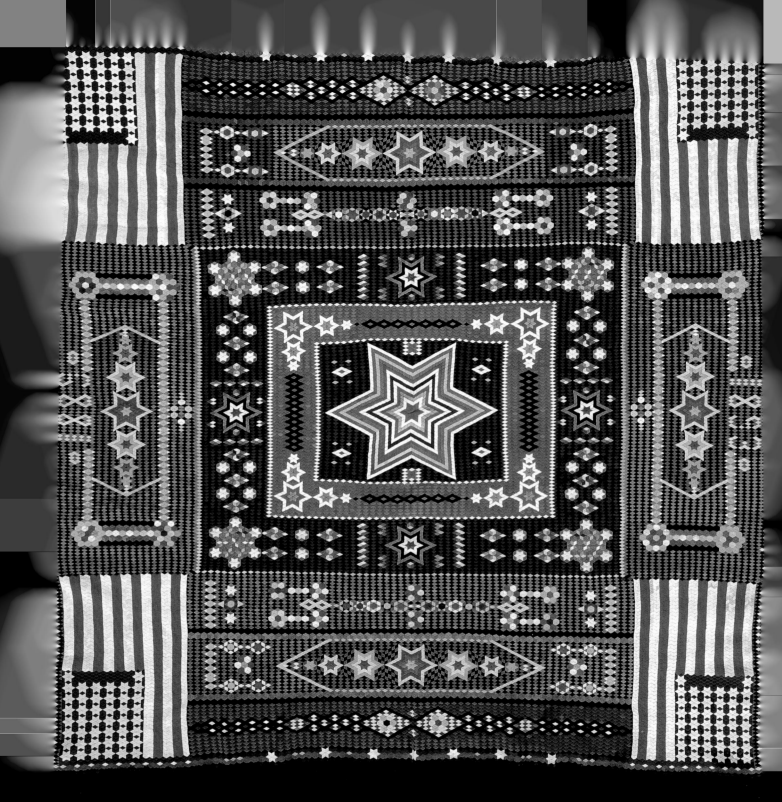

re 1-9 *Soldier's Quilt top, dated 1889 and 1893 in the piecing,*
tt Washington Curtis, Alaska; wool, pieced, 99" x 99", Collection of
Smithsonian Institution National Museum of American History,
hington D.C., 1984.0406.01, AQS 1557dc. Courtesy of the
hsonian Institution. The thousands of pieces in this quilt are less
one inch and some of the fabric may be from military uniforms.

A "Soldier's Quilt"

When Russian authority departed after the lowering of their double-eagle flag in Sitka, law and order was to be maintained in Alaska under a military command. The U.S. Army was active until 1877, and thereafter only a scattering of soldiers on special assignments were present until the late 1890s gold rush era.[29] The Victorian veneer of polite behavior wore thin when stampeders rushed into Alaska on their way to the Klondike gold fields of the Canadian Yukon. This wild stampede brought back the U.S. Army, and in turn created a quiltmaking puzzle.

On a visit to the textile storage rooms of the Smithsonian Institution National Museum of American History, steering committee member Mary Ann Vaughan was shown a quilt top made by Sergeant Jewett Washington Curtis (fig. 1.9). According to family stories, the quilt top was made in Alaska, and Sergeant Curtis became one of the most enigmatic quiltmakers. The survey decided to register his top as an important example of the many cultural items that have left Alaska in the perpetual ebb and flow of the boom and bust cycles that define the state's history.

Among various belongings, the quilt top emerged from a trunk inherited by Curtis' son. Sewn in the fashion of a British "Soldier's Quilt,"[30] Curtis used hand-piecing to assemble the many small bits of wool fabric. Traditionally, men recuperating from injuries, or serving sentences in military jails, made these elaborate quilts from the 1850s through WWI.[31] The typical fabric used for quilting came from soldiers uniforms. In the nineteenth century both girls and boys learned the rudiments of sewing, and Curtis was probably taught needlework skills at home. He may have learned the distinct style and intricate piecing of a "Soldier's Quilt" later in his long military career.

Curtis was born March 17, 1847 in Vermont. The Civil War had already begun its bloody course by 1862 when he was fourteen

Figure 1-10
Soldier's Quilt top detail, AQS 1557dc. Courtesy of the Smithsonian Institution.

years old and joined the U.S. Army. He became a musician in Company K, 104th Regiment New York Volunteer Infantry, popularly known as Wadsworth Guards. A mere five feet tall, Curtis drummed his troops into many battles including Antietam and Gettysburg where he was hospitalized briefly in July 1863.[32] Formally discharged from the Army in 1865, Curtis reenlisted in 1870 and began a protracted pattern of being in and out of service.

In the late 1880s, Curtis was stationed at Vancouver Barracks in Washington state. Mary Ann Putnam became his bride in 1895, and they tried farming at Mill Plain, Washington. The couple had three children; the oldest son, Clark, was the only survivor.[33] Worries connected to the rush for gold brought orders to the Vancouver Barracks to send an Alaska Relief Expedition and four companies from the 14th Infantry north to Alaska.[34] Curtis' Company B was shipped out by steamer and arrived in Skagway on March 8, 1898.[35] In the "interest of good order," they soon made camp near Dyea at the start of the Chilkoot Trail.

The troops were housed at first in large tents, and the monotony and ennui of camp life remained in strong contrast to the frenzy at Dyea. They played baseball and built a handball court to amuse themselves. Curtis would have had time on his hands for a project of a precise nature as he and fellow troops stood by. This seems an unlikely setting for quilt-making, but in fact, Dyea had become an instant town with almost all the amenities including "first class" hotels. In February 1898, the *Dyea Trail* reported a stock of woolen goods from the Minneapolis Woolen Mills valued at $8,000.[36] Some of this stock undoubtedly was fabric yardage. Quilt historian, Mary Bywater Cross, who has studied this quilt and its history extensively, says this particular wool fabric can not be solely identified as being used in military uniforms. Consistent quality and weight of cloth for uniforms was not common until later wars.[37] After fourteen months, Company B was relieved May 20, 1899 and most men were shipped south. Curtis was granted a requested discharge at this time.

The dates on the quilt top, 1889 and 1893, are dates which correspond to some of his known service at Vancouver Barracks with Company D, 14th Infantry. During that time Curtis was hospitalized for various causes including the amputation of one finger.[38] The American flags on the top have forty-four stars; Wyoming was admitted to the Union as the forty-fourth state in 1890. The reason these dates and the flags appear is unknown.

Figure 1-11 *CRAZY detail, dated 1898, unknown maker, possibly made in Kodiak, Alaska; cotton and silk, irregular pieced, 62" x 42", Mason family quilt collection, Wrangell Museum, AQS 676w. This embroidered motif of the "Midnight Sun" is unfinished. The quilt is one of only two nineteenth century quilts registered in the survey that is dated and inscribed with Alaska.*

If Curtis worked on the quilt top when he was at Dyea, he would have been in his early fifties. The top has a monumental quality and does not seem to be the first effort of a quilt-maker, but rather, a mature work of both control and inspiration. According to the family lore, this quilt top was displayed in a national fair and won a major prize. Two other pieced bedcovers are attributed to him. A smaller diamond-pieced quilt top used by Clark as a child is in the Abby Aldrich Rockefeller Folk Art Museum at Colonial Williamsburg, Virginia.[39]

After Curtis' wife died in 1904, young Clark went to live with his mother's sisters. The exact whereabouts of Curtis over the next several years are unknown; Clark and his father did not stay in contact. In the early 1920s, Curtis lived for a time in a veterans home in Orting, Washington.[40] Sometime late in life he became blind and after a short stay at the U.S. Soldiers' Home in Washington, D.C. died on March 30, 1927. The quilt top remains as a strong testament to Curtis' creative abilities.

Gold Rush Quilts

The discovery of gold in the Yukon and the nationwide economic depression in the 1890s started the greatest stampede since the California Gold Rush of 1849. The gold rush era of Alaskan quilt history coincides with the late nineteenth century changes in the attitudes towards women, their status and opportunities, and the ideas women developed about themselves. Martha Louise Black wrote about her adventures during the Yukon Gold Rush of 1898. "It looked like a great adventure and I was consumed with the urge to have my part in it."[41]

Women shared in the adventures, hardships, and successes of the far north. The women were of all ages, nationalities, marital status, and walks of life. The new roles for women in Alaska included those of miner and mine owner. Their writings reveal that the same motivations that brought men north also brought women to the Yukon and Alaska. The authors of *Gold Rush Women* concluded, "With

Figure 1-12 *LOG CABIN, 1865-1900, Helena Smith Sharp, possibly made in Missouri; cotton, velvet, wool, silk, pattern pieced, 63" x 76", Collection of Courtney Linkous, AQS 1035f. This gold rush quilt, backed with wool blanket pieces, was carried over the rugged Chilkoot Pass by the family in 1898. (See detail pp.16-17.)*

Figure 1-13 *Left to right: Quiltmaker Helena Smith Sharp holding her son, Ed Sharp, daughter, Margaret Smith, son, Adolphus Gustavus Smith and daughter, Clara Smith Bell. Courtesy of Courtney Linkous.*

a new sense of confidence and growing self-reliance, they not only survived but also flourished…. Because these women followed their dreams, not just of gold but of a life of greater independence and opportunity, their stories can inspire us today."[42]

Women have been stereotyped as home-loving creatures who did not want to leave family and friends for a life of hardship. Unfortunately, most historians assumed that the westward movement was predominately a male experience and also assumed that Alaska was settled mostly by males.[43] However, in 1890, the total white population in the District of Alaska consisted of 3,482 males and 3,196 females. Women made up 48 per cent of the white population before the Gold Rush of 1898.[44] The author of *Women of the American West*, Dr. Sandra Myres states, "Westering was not a male or a female experience, but a human experience."[45]

Plunging into the rush for gold caused families to abandon all but their most precious possessions. Like the pioneers of the Oregon Trail and the "forty-niners" of the California Gold Rush, the immigrants to Alaska brought quilts. The Log Cabin quilt top (*fig. 1.12*) made by Helena (Schaeffer) Smith Sharp was carried over the rugged Chilkoot Pass and down the Yukon River. Helena and her husband, "Harding" William Sharp, their son Edward, and Helena's three daughters Margaret, Clara, and Josephine Smith climbed the pass into the Yukon Territory in 1898 at the height of the gold rush. The family searched for gold and prospected the Stewart, White, and Forty Mile Rivers in Alaska. Prior to 1909, they traveled overland to the interior, settling in the mining camps of Cleary City and Dome City.[46] Helena sewed extensively and made numerous quilts. She died around 1920.[47]

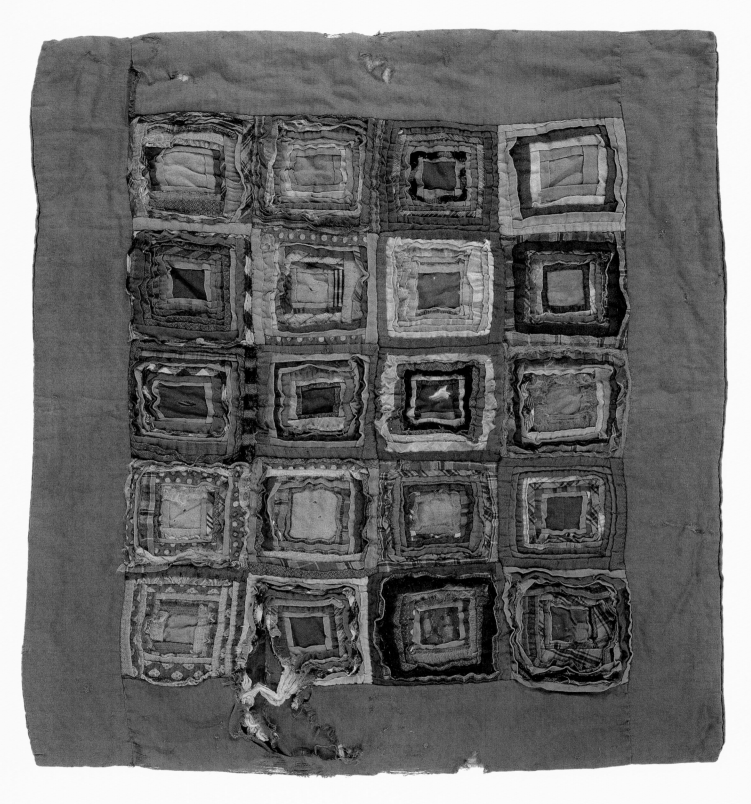

Figure 1-14 *LOG CABIN, 1865-1885, attributed to Frances (Charles) Waring or Jeanette (Waring) de Gruyter, possibly Kentucky; wool, pattern pieced, 33" x 30", Collection of the de Gruyter/ Hillery family, AQS 522sk. Skagway was a booming gold rush town when this much-used heirloom arrived with the family in 1898.*

Like men, women who came to the North wanted and needed their own kind of tools to help compete in the bustling frontier environment. "New Home" and "Jennie June" sewing machines were advertised in the Sitka newspaper, *The Alaskan*, in 1888.[48] As a matter of fact, forty sewing machines were in pre-Klondike Alaska and the Yukon.[49] In the early spring of 1894, Mrs. Anna DeGraf, a widow, hiked the Chilkoot Trail with her sewing machine. Anna said, "I took my sewing machine along, for I felt that I was going to an unknown land, where women and their work would be scarce, and it might be necessary for me to earn my living by sewing."[50] Just as Anna brought her sewing machine and fabric to the north, most of the documented nineteenth century quilts were brought to, rather than made in, Alaska.

The worn condition of quilts did not eliminate them from the items selected for the rush north. The much-used Log Cabin child's quilt *(fig. 1.14)* had sentimental value and warmed many babies before it came to the boom town of Skagway. The most likely maker was either Frances (Charles) Waring (1833-1895) or her daughter, Jeanette "Nettie" Ralston Waring. The family lived in Kentucky, and Nettie married Ferdinand J. de Gruyter in 1884. The couple had one daughter who was born in 1885, and named Jeanette Ralston de Gruyter.[51]

Ferdinand traveled to Skagway at the height of the Klondike Gold Rush of 1898, where he built a modest house for his family. He worked at Lee Guthrie's saloon at the gaming tables and had a reputation as an honest gambler.[52] Nettie and their thirteen-year-old daughter joined Ferdinand the following year. The quilt and the heirloom sewing kit *(fig. 1.16)* were probably brought to Skagway at that time. Frances Waring made the sewing kit and presented it to her daughter, Nettie, as a birthday gift when she turned thirteen. The kit is inscribed "Mamma to Nettie" and dated August 20, 1877. The handwritten note by Helen (one of Nettie's granddaughters), that accompanies the kit, says, "This sewing kit was made by my

Figure 1-15 *Jeanette "Nettie" (Waring) de Gruyter wearing a necklace made in Skagway of Klondike gold nuggets. Courtesy of the de Gruyter/Hillery family.*

Figure 1-16 *Sewing kit, dated Aug. 20, 1877; wool, Collection of the de Gruyter/Hillery family. On this sewing kit the date and inscription, "Mamma to Nettie", are embroidered with hair from the head of a family member.*

great grandmother [Frances] and given to her daughter, my grandmother [Nettie] on her birthday. Grandmother's mother [Frances] asked her to pull the gray hairs out of her head. Grandma [Nettie] wondered why. Then this birthday gift. Great Grandmother did this embroidery with her hair. I have used this ever since I was twenty years old. Helen." A Biblical reference to Rev. 3:12 is embroidered on the kit.[53]

Figure 1-17 *Vallie Wilson (left) and her older sister c.1908-10. Courtesy of Jane Scott Perkins.*

Figure 1-18 *CRAZY detail, 1910, Valerie "Vallie" Wilson and friends, North Carolina; cotton and wool, irregular pieced, 68" x 80", Collection of the Perkins family, AQS 1555n. Made as a wedding gift before Valerie married, and journeyed to Nome, with her new husband, Tolbert P. Scott.*

"Camp Quilts"

The second discovery of gold at Nome in 1899 in the sandy beaches brought another great rush of people to the northern edges of Alaska. This massive influx of people was on the wane when a quilt from North Carolina arrived in 1910 with newly wed Mrs. Valerie "Vallie" Scott. The quilt was begun by Vallie and her friends to commemorate her wedding to Tolbert P. Scott as well as to acknowledge their departure for Nome. Vallie was adventurous and willing to start a new life thousands of miles from her close family even though she realized she might only see her North Carolina family every ten years.

Vallie finished the quilt on her arrival in Nome and continued to make quilts for use in the family mining camps. She called them "camp quilts," a durable kind that added color to each bed. Her daughter wrote, "Mom and Dad never regretted their years in Nome… and never wanted to retire to the 'lower 48' as many seniors did. They always felt that although they never struck it rich with mining, it had been a good life and they were rich in family and friends and all they needed was a good cup of coffee and a game of pinochle to make the day complete."[54]

Ties and Dresses

Because Alaska was isolated from the rest of the United States, steamship travel was the major form of transportation to and from Alaska for decades. Alaska's coastal routes can be dangerous as evidenced by the large number of ship wrecks. A Crazy quilt *(fig. 1.20)* is associated with one of the famous steamship wrecks in Southeast Alaska. Venetia Lauretta Fehr was born in Tennessee in 1868. She came to Skagway, Alaska on the steamer *Seattle* in 1900 to teach school and returned to Oakland, California in December of that year to marry John Fraser Pugh. The couple soon returned to Alaska; and in 1904, their daughter was born in Ketchikan.[55]

John Pugh was appointed the U. S. Collector of Customs and stationed in Juneau with his family. On October 24, 1918, on a return trip from Skagway, the Canadian Pacific steamer *Princess Sophia* sank during a storm; John and the other passengers drowned. John was just forty-three years old at the time of his death.[56] Resouceful Venetia continued to live in Juneau and was employed as a Deputy Clerk of the U. S. Court.[57] She owned a tea shop along with Mrs. Jacob (Sophia) Britt.

In 1924, Venetia married Judge Thomas Milborn Reed in Seattle.[58] Mrs. Reed made her Crazy quilt *(fig. 1.20)* from ties and dresses she collected in Sitka, Juneau, Skagway, and Ketchikan. Some of the ties belonged to Dr. Mustard of Ketchikan. Venetia embroidered on the quilt the dates 1900 and 1930 which must have commemorated events in her life. In addition, she added her first husband's initials, JFP; R for Judge Reed; and the name Venetia Fraser Pugh. Venetia died at the Anchorage Pioneer's Home in 1967.[59]

The stories of Alaskan quilts are intertwined with the search for a Northwest Passage and the search for riches. Just as the fur and gold rushes brought men and women to Alaska, so were quilts and the quiltmaking tradition imported to the "Last Frontier." When the first quilt came to, or was made in, Alaska remains unknown. In spite of the long tradition of quiltmaking in both Russia and the United States, surprisingly few nineteenth century quilts were discovered. Nevertheless, the first person the survey identified as bringing quilts to Alaska was Libby Beaman in 1879. The 1888 Judge Dawson quilt is one of the first known Alaskan-made quilts. Once established, the art of quiltmaking continued to be practiced in Alaska, and its development followed the ebb and flow of the state's history.

Figure 1-19 SS Princess Sophia *telegram, 1918. Collection of Karl Austin Hahn, Jr. This was the only telegram to be sent before the sinking of the steamship off the coast of Southeast Alaska.*

Figure 1-20 *CRAZY detail, dated 1900 and 1930, Venetia (Fehr) Pugh Reed, possibly made in Juneau, Alaska; satin, velvet and silk, irregular pieced, 59" x 75", Collection of Karl Austin Hahn, Jr., AQS 960a. Venetia commemorated special events and people in her life with embroidered details and saved family fabrics.*

CHAPTER 2

TAKING COMFORT

June E. Hall

"I BROUGHT OUT OUR SOFT BOLSTER, slips for it, the large eiderdown that I quilted for my hope chest, and the crazy quilt which Sister Carrie and I made during that last care free summer vacation of hers, before she went back to Vassar and the diphtheria epidemic that took her away from us. I thought again poignantly of Carrie as I unpacked the vivid quilt. Should she have gotten married in her freshman year as she wanted to do? And if she had, what would her life have been like by now? Each brilliant scrap of silk—they are intricately feather stitched together, some embroidered or painted as fancies—is a memory of a ball or a party or a gala affair we attended, for the scraps are from our gowns and dresses. These are the gay, lovely memories I shall have to live on in this

(above left) **Figure 2-1** *Mary Catherine Jacob F. Grant seated with their childre the homestead outside Windom, Minne c.1898. Courtesy of Marjories G. Colpit*

(right) **Figure 2-2** *EIGHT POINTED S detail, c.1895-1900, Mary Catherine (Geddes) Grant, Windom, Minnesota, 71" x 88"; cotton, pattern pieced, Collection of Marjorie G. Colpitts, AQS 536p.*

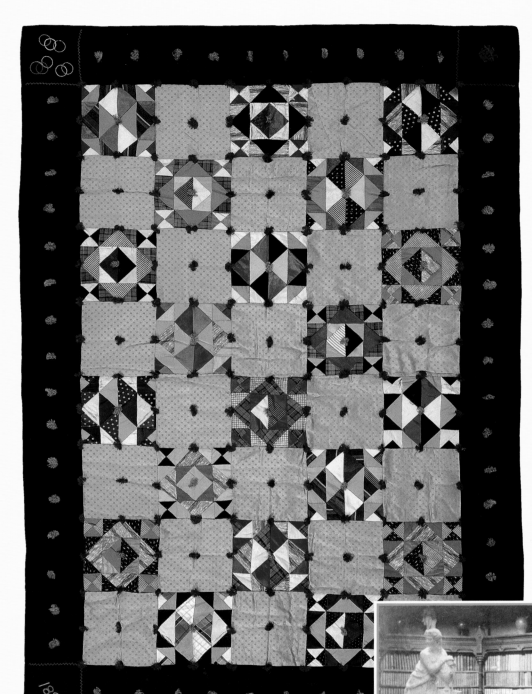

Figure 2-3 *MOSAIC variations, dated 1887, Catherine Monroe (March) Clark, Massachusetts; silk and satin, pattern pieced, 44" x 64", Collection of Pauline G. Wilson, AQS 1290f.*

Figure 2-4 *Catherine Monroe (March) Clark (1816-1893) in her Framingham, Massachusetts home. Courtesy of Pauline G. Wilson. Note the spinning wheel in this formal high Victorian setting.*

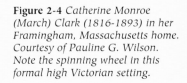

gloomy land of dirty skin coats and shapeless Mother Hubbards. Thank goodness, too I brought two irons!"[1]

Libby Beaman recorded these thoughts in 1879 just after she came ashore on the Pribilof Island of St. Paul in the vast expanse of the Bering Sea. Alaska must have seemed like a remote place then, as it does even now. Before one ventures to the far north, it is difficult to visualize the true landscape and great space. For Libby, the quilt she brought with her was a reservoir of feelings she did not want to leave behind. Her beloved sister came with her embodied in the quilt made of party-dress materials Carrie had worn in more light-hearted times. Familiar objects, like quilts, are all the more precious in a strange, distant place, and the memories they hold fill the voids of loneliness and uncertainty. Their quiet intimacy gives strength for dealing with the confusion of the unfamiliar.

Cloth Transformed

The majority of the quilts documented in the Alaska Quilt Survey were brought to Alaska as cherished heirlooms, and like Libby's quilt, they give comfort through time and space. A quilt, sewn from the same kind of party dress materials and made about the same date as Libby's quilt, was registered in Fairbanks (fig. 2.3). The clothing chosen for this quilt are colorfully rich and shiny smooth. After a hundred years, the fabrics still glow with a patterned warmth and vitality, seducing the eye to look at them. Catherine Monroe (March) Clark, the quiltmaker, was born in Massachusetts in 1816. According to notes written by a descendant, Catherine made this quilt from party dresses worn earlier by her, and possibly by her forty-one-year-old daughter Emily, who was well past her "party" days as well. As married women, they wore more subdued dark dresses.[2]

The use of clothing in making quilts is significant. The material chosen for any art object contributes not only to its form but to some of its content as well. Again and again at Discovery Days, quilt owners told about the

fabrics found in their quilts which had been aprons or shirts or dresses of family members or friends. Because these fabrics had been worn as clothing, they seem to have absorbed some of the life of the wearer. The makers of these quilts might have purchased the yardage needed to make them but chose instead to use familiar fabrics because they were a way of preserving the memory of a loved one. They also served a larger purpose—to preserve the life of feeling. These feelings are not the nostalgic sentiments associated with melodramatic moods but rather genuinely felt emotions upon which the inner life depends. This ability of quilts to contain and preserve the life of feeling is one of their most important functions, and one of many traditional purposes of art. For many quilt owners the fabric in their quilts served as visual reminders of other times and places. Certain elements of the visual world impress themselves upon the mind's eye and become visual memories. Often these visual impressions enter in a subtle, unconscious manner. Patterned house dress material casually seen everyday in the kitchen becomes associated with warmth and security, or the fabrics of play clothes become the endless summer of childhood. After touching and seeing, wearing and washing, folding and unfolding this fabric, a tactile connection is made that the hands and mind do not forget. Ordinary cloth is ordinary no longer when transformed into an artfully quilted object of pattern and color.

More than once the survey's Discovery Day participants told about how the act of quiltmaking itself had served to comfort. The soft material for quilts can be cut and shaped easily with the hands. Individual pieces of color arranged into a fabric mosaic can be picked up and moved about. The rhythm of hands sewing small soft pieces unleashes thoughts, or provides for a release from thoughts — sometimes a needed numbing of the mind. A bed quilt when finished makes an association with the human body for its scale is determined by the proportions of the human figure.

Figure 2-5 *Newspaper clipping of unknown origin. Courtesy of the Barrow Morgan family.*

(below) **Figure 2-6** *GRANDMOTHER'S FLOWER GARDEN detail, Mae (Quinlan) Post, dated and signed 1938, Mrs. W. F. Post, age 65, Maysville, Okla.; cotton, pieced, 72" x 81", Collection of Donna and Barrow Morgan, AQS 1556n.*

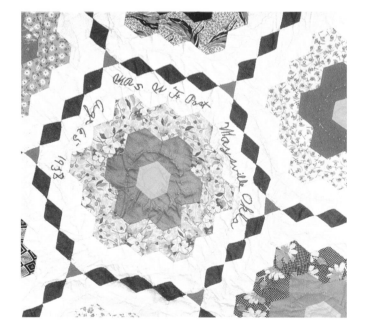

Commemorating a Hero

Mae (Quinlan) Post of Oklahoma surely needed the solace offered by the act of quilt-making after she lost her famous son, Wiley Post, in a plane crash on August 15, 1935. Going down in the plane with Wiley was Will Rogers, one of America's favorite commentators on the humorous side of life. The men were on an adventurous trip around the world when their small plane crashed just outside of Point Barrow, Alaska. Mrs. Post made the quilt *(fig. 2.6)* for Sergeant Stanley Morgan, the man she felt had done so much for her during this traumatic time. An Eskimo family at their hunting camp witnessed the crash; Clair Okepeaha ran with the news fifteen miles to Point Barrow. "It was Sergeant Morgan, who, in charge of the army radio station at Point Barrow, outpost of civilization in the far north, gave to the outside world the first word of the tragedy.... It was he who assembled the group of Eskimos to accompany him up the ice-filled river in an open whaling boat to the scene of the crash. It was he who took charge of convey-ing the bodies to the mission hospital at Point Barrow. Finally, it was he who sent out to the grieved and waiting world a detailed account of the accident, and of what had been done." Wiley's parents did not have a telephone on their small farm at the time of the crash and their lone radio, where they kept track of their son's adventure, was not working.[3]

At the funeral "Mrs. W. F. Post, Wiley's white-haired mother, left the church aided by

Figure 2-7 *William and Mae Q. Post pose with a portrait of their heroic son, Wiley, shortly after his death in 1935. Photograph courtesy of the* The Daily Oklahoman, *Oklahoma City.*

(above) **Figure 2-9** *POPPY detail, quilt signed and dated "Z 1942," Mary S. Zaldaris (Marjona S. Zaldariene), Pennsylvania; cotton, whole top appliqué, 74" x 88", Collection of Edmund Zaldaris, AQS 53j. This poppy design was a popular published pattern from 1920s-1950s.*

(right) **Figure 2-8a-b** *RED WORK details, Mary S. Zaldaris, dated and signed, "Marjona Zaldariene, 1905, Tusmetus Geguziaus 1 diena Coaldale Pa Box 48," Pennsylvania; cotton, pieced, 84" x 88", Collection of Edmund Zaldaris, AQS 51j.*

two national guard officers. 'My darling's gone. My darling boy is gone,' she cried."[4] Three years after the accident Wiley's mother finished the quilt for Sergeant Morgan, embroidered the date and her name on it, and mailed it to Point Barrow. The carefully cut pieces of each "flower" revealed her desire to focus on every tiny patterned petal. The Post family also sent bicycles to Point Barrow for Sergeant Morgan's two children; they were the first bicycles in that isolated Eskimo village. From experience, Mae Post knew how to get through hard times. She, her husband and their older children had been itinerant farm workers in the Midwest and Texas just before Wiley's birth. They continued to live in the region hardest hit by the Dust Bowl. (No quilts made by Mae Post appeared in the Oklahoma quilt documentation project.)

Northern European Roots

Leaving family quilts behind never occurred to most people who had moved to Alaska and

registered quilts in the survey. They often carried them from place to place for years. Anna Wenzel came to the first Discovery Day in Juneau with her arms full of family quilts. Her step was unsure, but she was firm in her belief that her mother's quilts were worthy to be registered. This pride was justified, especially for the Red Work embroidered quilt (fig. 2.8) with its simple folk designs. Anna brought most of these quilts with her when she moved to Alaska in 1949. Alaska was a territory, and she worked as an traveling nurse among the "bush" villages. At the beginning of the twentieth century, her mother Mary (Marjona Stanelis Zaldariene) Zaldaris (1878-1957) emigrated from Lithuania to America and settled in Eastern Pennsylvania, at Coaldale. She came as a teenaged bride; for some reason, her desire to learn quiltmaking met resistance among the local quiltmakers. Undaunted, she taught herself. The Red Work quilt, her first effort, was finished in 1905. The

delightful designs are in the northern European folk tradition and provided a connection to her homeland so far away. As if taking pride in her new American home, Mary put her address in Pennsylvania along the border, and even included the post office box. She made many more quilts, and forty years later she finished the exquisitely sewn Poppy appliqué quilt (fig. 2.9). Even though Mary used a commercial pattern, the quilt shows the same concern for details and the love of bold design displayed in her first quilt. Her embroidered threads texture the flower details as subtly as nature itself.

Bridging Generations

Special connections are made through quilts — intangible connections made manifest in soft quilted materials held together by stitches like tiny threads around the heart. The scissors motif appearing on the Crazy quilt (fig. 2.10), made by Fannie (Davidson) Scroggs, connects three generations. Fannie was born in Texas in 1878 and died giving birth when she was only twenty-two years old. She loved animals, especially horses, and they loved her. Fannie's granddaughter now owns the quilt and wrote this short history about her. "[My] Mother died at age eighty-four. Her mother [Fannie] died when she was two years old. All her life, my mother placed the scissors emblem on every craft project that she made. It appeared on her mother's quilts."[5] Fannie's autograph album has been saved, and reveals a glimpse of her and her times: "Honor and fame from low condition rise, Act well your part there all the honor lies. Papa" Another is more humorous, "Dear Fannie, May your virtue ever spread like butter on hot gingerbread. Your true friend B. Ellie Gibson, Lancaster Aug. 23, [18]92."

Figure 2-10 *CRAZY top detail, c.1896, Fannie Laura (Davidson) Scroggs, Texas; silk, wool and cotton, irregular pieced and appliquéd, 52" x 71", Collection of Betty Ames, AQS 1201ke.*

Figure 2-11 *Fannie Laura (Davidson) Scroggs, c.1896. Courtesy of Betty Ames.*

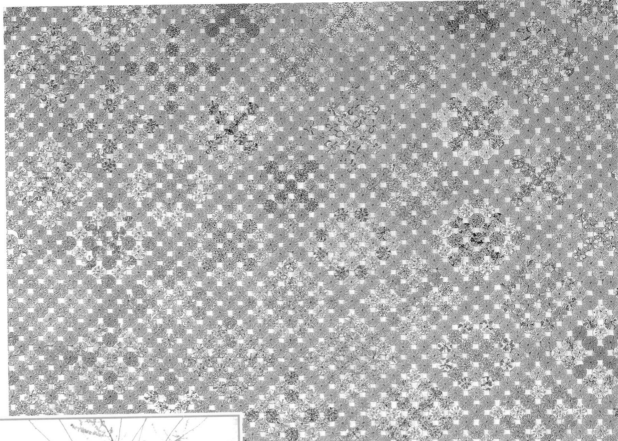

Figure 2-12 *YO-YO, c.1934, Ura Birdie (Conkle) Mills, Garden Grove, California; cotton, pattern pieced, 88" x 100", Collection of Leslie M. Hamilton. AQS 1212ke.*

Figure 2-13 *Ura Birdie (Conkle) Mills (left) and family on their fruit farm in Garden Grove, California. Courtesy of Leslie M. Hamilton.*

California Colors

Ura Birdie (Conkle) Mills chose the popular Yo-yo style *(fig. 2.12)* for a quilt made about 1934. Ura was born in Ohio in 1881 and moved to Santa Ana, California as a child. The mellow, warm colors and circular shapes used in the quilt are reminiscent of the colors and shapes Ura saw every day of her life in California. Leslie Mills Hamilton, a granddaughter of the maker, remembers seeing the quilt on the bed as a little girl, and after her own marriage the quilt was given to her. The same determination needed to finish a large Yo-yo quilt also helped Ura after she lost her husband; she continued to manage their orange orchard in Garden Grove, California and raise her three children. Though far from its original setting in a California farm house, the quilt and the walnut bed for which it was made are still together in Kenai.

Figure 2-14 *Flora (Rhodes) Corbin (1863-1948) in the 1930s with one version of her many appliqué and pieced U.S. map quilts. Courtesy of Selma Giesler.*

Uniting a Far-flung Family

A woman who never came to Alaska left behind many quilts which still unite a far-flung family. Flora Cecilia (Rhodes) Corbin (1863-1948) was an exceptionally skilled quiltmaker from Wisconsin; she always seemed to be in the process of making quilts. Granddaughter, Selma Geisler, in Roundup, Montana relates that Flora was "fussy" about the quality of her sewing "even one stitch."[6] Flora's mother before her was a quiltmaker. Flora seemed to have a sense of her place within the quilt-making tradition and wanted to pass on her craft legacy. Selma remembers Flora teaching her to sew the beginner's Nine Patch as a young girl.

Flora married William Perry Corbin, and in 1909 they moved from Illinois to homestead in Montana. Their family eventually included six girls and two boys. Still Flora found time to make quilts, and in fact, made a series of U.S. map quilts in the 1930s, giving at least six versions to her children. Her daughter Wilma moved to Wrangell, Alaska in 1924, and Flora

Figure 2-15 *GARDEN PATH detail, 1900-1925, Flora (Rhodes) Corbin, possibly Montana; rayon, pattern pieced, 72" x 74", Mason family quilt collection, Wrangell Museum, Wrangell, Alaska, AQS 672w.*

wrote her there: "I have my wedding ring quilt just about done, ready for lining and quilting. I expect Ora to furnish that for the quilt is for Kenneth. Ora has furnished nearly everything for it. It sure is pretty. Want to finish my U. S. quilt next." [7] Flora was living in Illinois at the time and apparently entered one of her map quilts in the 1933 Chicago Century of Progress Exposition quilt competition sponsored by Sears, Roebuck and Company; almost 25,000 quilts were entered. [8] The quilts were submitted through the company stores and mail order offices where they were first judged. The family still keeps Flora's individual state cardboard templates for these map quilts, and her quilting frame.

Wilma remained in Alaska and though she liked to sew, she never made quilts. She and her mother mailed other kinds of needle-work suggestions back and forth. Wilma inherited Flora's Garden Path *(fig. 2.15)* which is richly sewn with rayon fabrics to create a dark garden of midnight blossoms. Flora's Tumbling Block quilt *(fig. 2.16)* incorporates a "crazy" style of piecing within the blocks for another strong visual effect. Flora painted flowers in watercolors, and the many varieties embroidered on this quilt show a careful observation of nature. Wilma's son, Ken Mason, had these quilts brought into the Discovery Day in Wrangell; later from his attic storage boxes, Flora's story unfolded.

Delicate Gifts

One of the most difficult things about moving to Alaska is the long separation from friends and family, and dealing with the great distance between. Marcia Healy came to Alaska on a vacation and never moved back to the "lower 48." Marcia keeps her grandmother close

Figure 2-16 *TUMBLING BLOCK detail, 1900-1925, Flora (Rhodes) Corbin, possibly Montana; velvet, satin and silk, pattern pieced, 52" x 67", Mason family quilt collection, Wrangell Museum, Wrangell, Alaska, AQS 657w.*

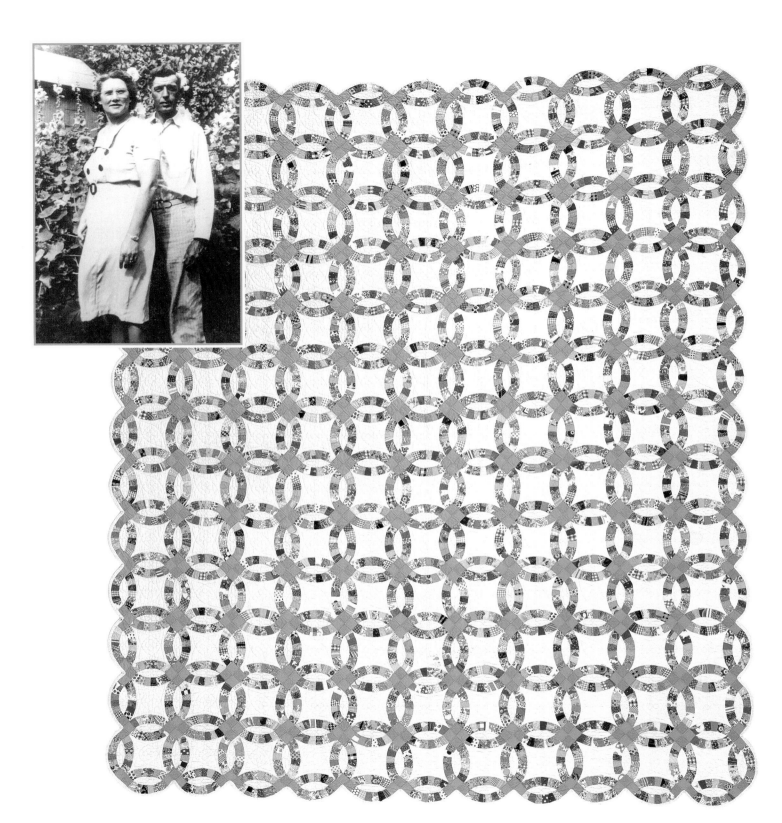

Figure 2-17 *Driekie (Van Rootselaar) Vriezelaar (1898-1999) and her husband, James, in the 1940s. Courtesy of Marcia Healy.*

Figure 2-18 *DOUBLE WEDDING RING, c.1979, Driekie (Van Rootselaar) Vriezelaar, Iowa; cotton, pattern pieced, 78" x 100", Collection of Marcia Healy, AQS 461h.*

through her quilts. Driekie (Van Rootselaar) Vriezelaar (1898-1999) was of Dutch descent and eventually settled in Iowa with her husband. Most of her quilts were made as gifts to family members. They are not spectactular quilts of sophisicated design but rather unpretentious, honest efforts, carefully crafted. The real gift she gave was not so much the quilt itself, but the time and effort she was willing to spend in making that gift. The gentle but strong rhythm of the small, intertwining rings of her Wedding Ring quilt *(fig 2.18)* are beautiful in their consistency. Her clear but subtle colors and careful attention to detail harmonize into an overall effect of delicate structure not to be unraveled.

Puzzle Pieces of Lives

Sometimes all we inherit from ancestors are a few puzzle pieces of their lives. A letter edged in black, a few unfinished quilt pieces, patterns, bobbins, and lace were items Terri Zacher found in the trunk of her great-great grandmother, Martha (McCoy) Jones (1858-1912). With these items, Terri added another generation of quilted items to the four generations she already possessed. "How lucky can you be?" she marveled. Terri had heard from her family that Martha had beautiful black hair and eyes, but since she never allowed her photograph to be taken, the mementos in the trunk would have to illustrate her story. Martha was born in Tiplersville, Mississippi and became a woman of deep religious convictions. It is known that she married John Winston Jones in 1875 and had eleven children. The humility of her strung-together triangles of scrap material speak of her desire to salvage and save *(fig. 2.19)*. Some of these small pieces are themselves pieced together, evidence of the enforced frugality of her life. As a farm wife, she didn't leave much of herself when she died, but her descendants are loving and close, Terri related. They follow the steady course she set so many years before.[9]

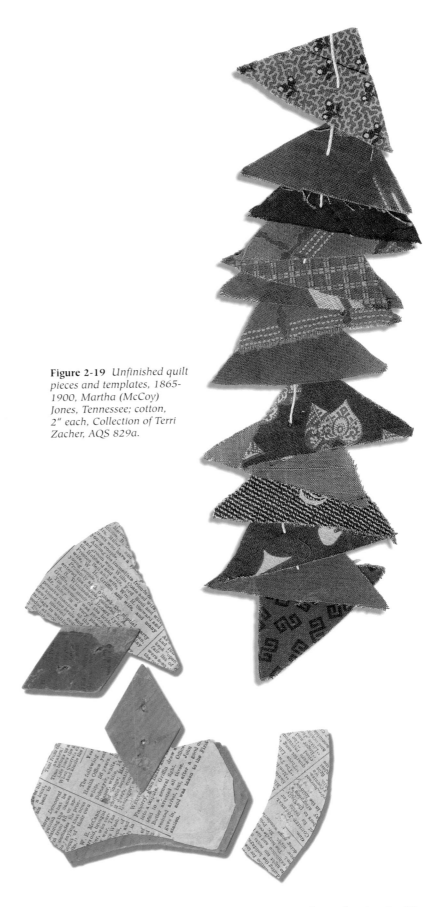

Figure 2-19 *Unfinished quilt pieces and templates, 1865-1900, Martha (McCoy) Jones, Tennessee; cotton, 2" each, Collection of Terri Zacher, AQS 829a.*

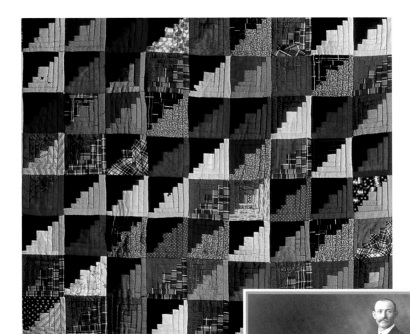

Figure 2-20 *LOG CABIN detail, 1902, Mabel (Allen) Spence, New Brunswick, Canada; wool and cotton, pattern pieced, 58" x 76", Collection of Will and Anne Harrison, AQS 1063f.*

A Worrier, a Comedian and a Tease

Some quilts in the survey traveled not only the long miles from another state to Alaska, but came from another country. The Log Cabin quilt *(fig. 2.20)* was made in New Brunswick, Canada and came to Alaska with a grandson of the maker. In 1902, when Mabel Louise (Allen) Spence was pregnant, she worked on this quilt as a gift for her new baby. A hand-written biography by her daughter, Thelma, captures with a direct style the details and essence of her mother's life. "Mabel's youth was something less than a happy one. No doubt their mother's early death when Mabel was seven and [her brother] Maunsell five was more emotionally upsetting to the sensitive children than anyone realized. Mabel, being the first born, had much of the care of her father's second family, not because her little stepmother shirked, but because there was so much work to be done. The Allen homestead, being conveniently located with the welcome mat out to all comers, became a free inn. But it was not the hard work in itself that was so dispiriting for this fun-loving girl. What was so disheartening was being deprived of a chance for recreation, of the opportunity to enjoy life with other young people. All through her years she remembered with bitterness not having been allowed to attend the young people's dances. While her young friends were having fun Mabel was helping with the children, and waiting on her sick uncle and on the family's nonpaying guests. It is not surprising that in later years Mabel often used to say, 'Having had no young life, I can never grow old gracefully.'"[10]

(right) **Figure 2-21** *Mabel (Allen) Spence (seated) with her daughter, Thelma and her husband Clarence. Courtesy of Will and Anne Harrison.*

(below) **Figure 2-22** *Handwritten biographical manuscript (c.1975) of Mabel (Allen) Spence by her daughter Thelma. Collection of Will and Anne Harrison.*

MABEL (ALLEN) SPENCE

Mabel's lively imagination and her love of her fellows made a walk on a busy street a pleasurable experience. Snatches of conversation made it interesting to speculate on people's personalities, their homes, and their work. Her hobby was people. Her practice of observing hands was another method of forming a mental picture of their characteristics and environment. The first thing most people notice about a person is his face; the first thing Mabel always noticed was his hands. Were they soft, or were they calloused? Were they smooth, or were they wrinkled? Were they long and slender, or were they stubby? To her a person's hands told much about that person; to her they were a label.

A worrier, a comedian and a tease seems an unlikely combination, but that was Mabel. She had what was almost a gift, the knack of being able to dramatize little incidents making them very amusing. And she had a penchant for teasing. Even the animals were subject. For instance the cat, the kittens, the pig, and the hens were all likely to be held a moment by their tails!

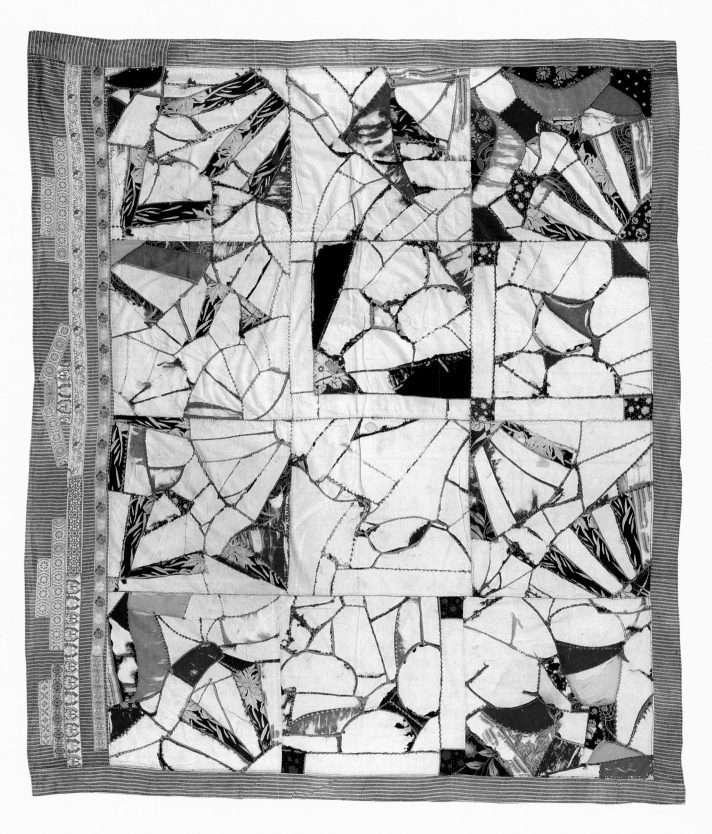

Figure 2-23 *CRAZY, 1880-1900, unknown maker; wool, silk and cotton, irregular pieced, 78" x 94", Collection of Cheri Wickman, AQS 649w. This "all gone" Crazy quilt, or what is left of it, is a visual mystery from a distance. The dark shreds of fabric left along the seams create a delicate structure against the white ground, like pencil lines in a Cubist drawing.*

Mabel's intelligence and ambition were recognized by her local clergyman and his wife, and they helped her attend school. Eventually she received a teaching certificate and taught at three different country schools in New Brunswick. At the third, in Spence settlement, she met her future husband Clarence.[11]

Though Mabel worried about "growing old gracefully", the careful arrangement of her Log Cabin design, the thoughtfulness of the fabric selection, and the precise piecing of her quilt reveal her ability and desire to bring order and beauty into both her life and that of her unborn child. Her quilt, and every quilt, is a visual and tactile biography if studied carefully.

Keepsakes

Keeping quilts as memorials was important for several survey participants. They kept the quilts with them as they would keep an old friend company. Claude Klaver brought in a quilt which "was made by my best friend,

Louis King, who died suddenly at age 25. His mother gave the blocks to me. My mother sewed it and had it quilted in the early fifties. I have had it since. Louis made the quilt blocks sometime as a boy. I knew nothing about it 'til after his death…[he was] my best friend beside my wife, that I have ever had."[12]

Being the keeper of a family quilt was a responsibility that many survey participants took seriously. A carefully preserved Whig Rose and Carolina Lily quilt *(fig. 2.24)* was brought to a Juneau Discovery Day by the great-great-great granddaughter of the maker. A note attached to the quilt read, "Dear Dorothy, I am sending you and Warren this lovely Bed Spread over a hundred years old that my grandmother Goodell left to me in her will — 'because she had observed that I took care of things'. So I am giving it to you and Warren to care for—She died in 1874 and was 70 years old—You must have a nice old four poster for it — I simply love it—It gives such color to a room. I am sorry not to see you married but it is quite impossible for us to get away…. Affectionately Frances Goodell Strong"[13]

Dorothy was married in 1922, and the quilt she received from her mother, Frances, could have been made as early as 1822. The quiltmaker, Hannah Griswold, was born in 1804 and married in 1820 in Mentor, Ohio. Her husband, Nathan Goodell, was a wool manufacturer and later a flour miller. The fine quilting and double-pink fabric in the roses show very little wear, revealing the care past generations have taken with it. This quilt is a material sign of the desire among the women of this family to preserve their ties. Because each generation knew how to "take care of things," the quilt undoubtedly will give comfort to many future generations.

Figure 2-24 *WHIG ROSE and CAROLINA LILY, c.1822, Hannah (Griswold) Goodell, Ohio; cotton, pattern pieced and appliqué, 87" x 90", Collection of Anne Fuller. AQS 74j. This quilt has very fine hand quilting.*

Figure 2-25 *Brian Ronald Dwight Eisenhauer with his parents, Ron and Ann, in Colorado around 1962. Courtesy of Larry and Lynnette L. Motz.*

Figure 2-26 *ROCKY ROAD TO KANSAS, 1944, Anna Maria (Biehn) Sames, Coopersburg, Pennsylvania; cotton, pattern pieced, 84" x 97", Collection of Larry and Lynnette L. Motz, AQS 900a.*

Brian's Quilt

Certain quilts lead to stories of a special kind. The brief history of "Brian's quilt" *(fig. 2.26)* was gathered from Ann Eisenhauer and written for us by the owner, Lynnette L. Motz. "When the Eisenhauer brothers came to America, two of the brothers changed the spelling of the family name to Eisenhower, the others did not. Obviously, Brian's ancestors kept the German spelling, but the family still remained in contact over the generations. When President Dwight D. Eisenhower was hospitalized in Denver, [his brother] Ronald took his wife Ann and young Brian for a get-well visit. Brian presented the President with a gift of golf balls.

"Mrs. Leo (Anna Marie) Sames of Coopersburg, Pennsylvania made this quilt in the mid-1940s for her great-grandson, Brian Ronald Dwight Eisenhauer. Brian (the only kid in school with four names) was a classmate and a good friend of mine — the only child of Ron and Ann. Brian was tragically killed at age eighteen in an automobile accident. When I married Larry Motz in 1963, Ann gave me the quilt at my bridal shower — a gift we treasure to this day."[14] The quiltmaker, Anna Sames, was born in Germany in 1861 and died in 1948.

Figure 2-27 VARIABLE STAR, 1927, Marie Downs, Spokane, Washington; cotton, pattern pieced, 14" x 18", Collection of Patty Bickar. AQS 406s. This doll quilt is the second version after the first was lost in the mail.

Once Familar Fantasy World

Making a quilt for a child's doll lets a quiltmaker re-enter a world of once familiar fantasy. Each miniature piece becomes part of a mysterious world the maker once inhabited. In 1927, as a gift for Patty Robert's first Christmas, Marie Downs bought a doll and made a quilt for it. She sent the quilt and doll through the mail, but the gift never reached Patty. Marie bought a second doll and made a new quilt *(fig. 2.27)* which arrived for Patty's birthday in March of 1928. The doll has long since worn out, but the quilt remains to comfort another generation of dolls.[15]

Several of the quilts documented in the survey were finished many years after they were first started. Some quilts were finished by family; some finished by complete strangers. The completion of a single work of art by different people over several generations is highly unusual in the Western tradition of art. This familial and communal way of making quilts conflicts with the Western concept of the single artist laboring in isolation. This way of working and thinking about quilts is very different from that found in the other "fine" arts. Most often other quiltmakers felt it was their "duty" to complete the quilts. In this way, the quilts served to bind people together, and new identities were bound in with the old. It would be rare for a descendant of a painter or sculptor to complete a predecessor's work, or even add to it.

Figure 2-28 Marie Downs (left) with her son, Tom and (right) Cora Roberts with her grandchildren, Leslie and Patty Roberts and Virginia Wheatley in Spokane, Washington, c.1928. Courtesy of Patty (Roberts) Bickar.

Figure 2-29 *MISSOURI BEAUTY, 1914, Elizabeth R. Kunkel, Evelyn Kunkel, Emma V. Kuhns and Eliza A. Kunkel, Newpoint, Missouri; cotton, pieced and appliqué, 87" x 87", Collection of Phyllis Kunkel Davis, AQS 139j.*

Missouri Beauty

The red and green appliqué quilts American quiltmakers so loved to make often were for something "special," and the effort in their making was often shared. Elizabeth (Robinson) Kunkel chose this style for a quilt to commemorate the 1914 birth of her great granddaughter and namesake, Inez Elizabeth Kunkel (Roberts). The quilt *(fig. 2.29)* is unusual in its construction, as Elizabeth used very precise straight stitching with a pedal sewing machine to secure the appliqué pieces. At Newpoint, Missouri the quilt took shape with the help of Inez's mother, Evelyn Kunkel, who set the blocks together by hand. Inez's grandmothers, Emma V. Kuhns and Eliza A. Kunkel did the quilting. The quilt came to Alaska with a great-great granddaughter who cherishes its beauty and also makes her own quilts.[16]

Figure 2-30 *RISING SUN, 1934, Maude (Kidd) Steele, Leanna Kidd, Geneva Lee (Steele) Martens, Pebworth, Kentucky; cotton, pattern pieced, 79" x 82", Collection of the Martens Family, AQS 812a. For the second time in two years, the skillful execution of a Hubert Ver Mehren (Home Art Studios) complexly-designed kit quilt was chosen as a major prize winner. In 1933, Lillie Carpenter won first prize with this design in the Philadelphia regional quilt contest for the Sears Chicago Century of Progress Exposition. In 1934, this quilt won a grand prize in Detroit. Susie Combs from Pebworth, Kentucky who had won an honorable mention in the Philadelphia contest, was a quilting friend of the Steele family.*

The Rising Sun

A truly unexpected find at the Anchorage Discovery Days was an prize-winning quilt made by three generations of women. It exemplifies the cooperative nature of creating quilts and the beauty that results. The Rising Sun quilt *(fig. 2.30)* won the grand prize in the second annual 1934 *The Detroit News* Quilt Club contest and is important to American quilt history. Quilt contests during the 1930s were hugely popular; enthusiasm ran high for this one as evidenced by the hundreds of women who waited long hours before the doors officially opened.

The quiltmaker, Mrs. Maude (Kidd) Steele, was from Pebworth, Kentucky, an area known for its fine quilters. The newspaper reported that when she came to receive her prize money of $100, it "was her first trip to a big city but her poise…was not shaken by the fact that more than 50,000 persons visited the Quilt Show in the Naval Armory and stood in admiration before her rising sun pattern prize quilt."[17] Maude was amazed at the attention she received and at being dubbed the "Quilt Queen," as she considered herself a simple country woman. "She attended the exhibit Friday, the opening day, but did not make herself known to anyone in charge, in the sincere belief that no one really wanted to see or talk to her. All Saturday evening WWJ broadcast requests for information regarding the possible whereabouts of the 'Quilt Queen' in Detroit." Eventually, her relatives took her to the sponsoring newspaper headquarters in the Armory.[18]

When the Quilt Club honored her in 1934, Maude was forty-six. A photograph appearing with the newspaper story that described her accomplishments shows a dark-haired, modestly-smiling woman looking down at a doily she is embroidering. Maude's husband, W. S. Steele, was a "thrifty farmer who deals in saddle horses," but the major work in the Steeles' neat brown frame farmhouse was quilting. Maude was taught quilting by her mother, Leanna Kidd, long years before. Maude

THE DETROIT NEWS, TUESDAY, OCTOBER 16, 1934.

Quilt Queen Happy and Busy

—By News Staff Photographer.
MRS. W. S. STEELE, the Quilt Queen of the second annual exhibit of The Detroit News Quilt Club, has ample reason to be happy. Winning the grand prize of $100 for her rising sun pattern quilt was a genuine thrill for this club member who lives in Pebworth, Ky. While visiting her sister, Mrs. Lillian Chumley, 17593 Orleans street, she keeps busy writing the good news back home to her 16-year-old daughter, Geneva, and embroidering doilies.

Figure 2-31 *RISING SUN detail, Collection of the Martens Family, AQS 812a. The hand quilting on this quilt measures fourteen stitches to the inch. (Also see previous page.)*

Figure 2-32 *Newspaper clipping about Maude (Kidd) Steele. The Detroit News, October 16, 1934. Collection of the Martens Family.*

also originated patterns, including the Rattlesnake, now known to quilters as Baby Bunting, the paper reported. Neighbors sometimes walked miles over the Cumberland foothills to meet, "swap" pieces of fabric, or hold quilting bees. All the household arts she so quietly took for granted are achievements in themselves, the newspaper went on to say, and then offered to its readers Maude's prize-winning recipe for corn bread. Geneva Lee, the Steele's daughter, aged sixteen, had "ambitions to become a queen of quilters some day."[19] She had worked on the Rising Sun quilt, as had Maude's mother.

Figure 2-33 *Georgia S. and Joshua E. Ingalls, c.1877. Courtesy of Marjorie G. Colpitts.*

grandmother Georgia Sanderson lived, it was the local custom for girls to sew quilt blocks from the scrap material of their new dresses. These blocks were given to boys that they "liked." When they married, these blocks were supposed to be sewn together by their wives! Before Georgia married Joshua Ingalls about 1877, he had received many pieced Album blocks. Joshua was a popular fellow and had enough blocks for two quilts. Georgia added the names of the makers in ink to the blocks and sewed one set together to make a quilt. Majorie related that over the years this quilt was "used up." Georgia had accidentally spilled ink on some of the other blocks and they were only sewn into a top. The top was put away in a trunk.

After World War I, Marjorie's great grandmother, Phoebe Sanderson, came to Minneapolis to help care for Georgia who was ill. To keep busy, she took the Album quilt top out of the trunk and replaced the ink-stained blocks. She added a "double-pink" border from fabric which had been commercially repro-duced to match the "old time" style. Flour sacking was the only material available to Phoebe for the backing. In the 1950s, it was quilted by a group of church women.[20]

Rare Flowers

Georgia's daughter (Marjorie's mother) Ruth, continued the family tradition of quilt-making. She married Charles Grant in 1904 and later moved to Oregon. *The Oregonian* newspaper (Portland) published a weekly quilt column in the 1930s, and Ruth used the appliqué pat-terns from this column for her quilt shown in figure 2.36. She added embroidered details to the flowers, which include bluebells, fuschia and poinsettias.

Spilled Ink

The people who came to Discovery Days often gave lessons in living by their presence alone, and Marjorie Colpitts, at the lively age of 90, was one of them. She had recently cleared out her large home in Oregon and moved to Petersburg, Alaska to live near her daughter. With her were generations of family quilts, including the first Crazy quilt she started at age 10 and many of the quilts of her mother and grandmothers. The quilts of her family were very tightly sewn together, not only by small stitches, but by their shared effort. An Album quilt with signature blocks *(fig. 2.34)* involved two generations of the family and was created through a custom that may no longer seem "romantically correct." Marjorie relates that in the small Wisconsin community where her

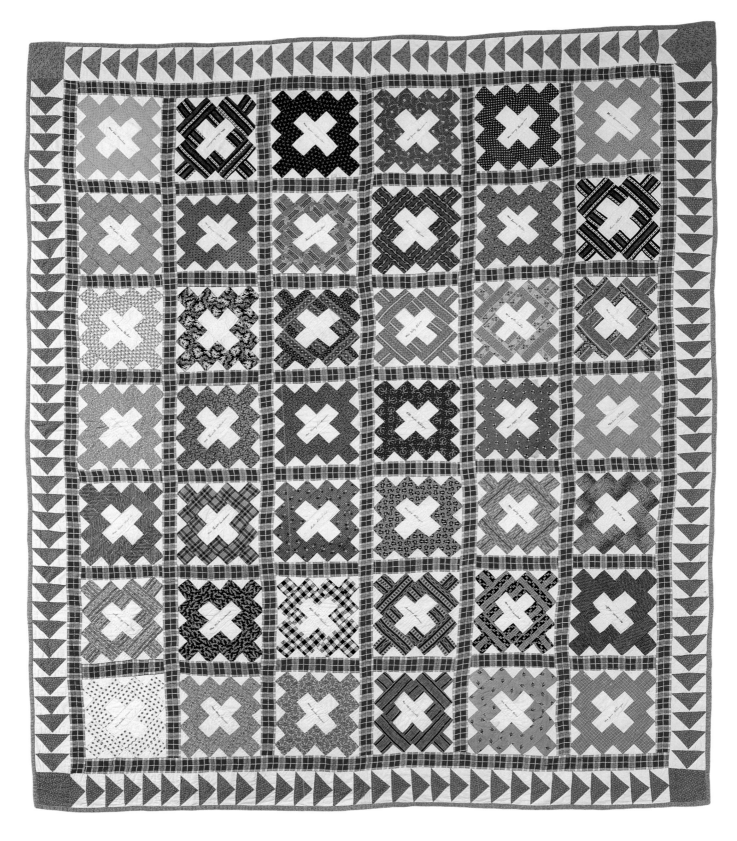

Figure 2-34 *ALBUM/ROMAN CROSS, 1875-1950,*
Georgia S. Ingalls and Phoebe Sanderson, Wisconsin
and Minnesota; cotton, pattern pieced, 73" x 84",
Collection of Marjorie G. Colpitts, AQS 540w.

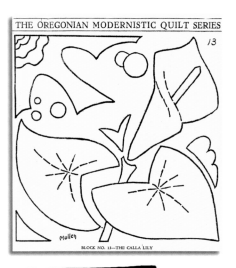

THE OREGONIAN MODERNISTIC QUILT SERIES

13

Mullen

BLOCK NO. 13—THE CALLA LILY

(right) **Figure 2-36 a** *Pattern Block No.13-The Calla Lily, Modernistic Flower quilt. From the Mildred Dickerson Collection owned by Merikay Waldvogel.*

(below) **Figure 2-36 b** *MODERNISTIC FLOWER, 1933-1934, Ruth (Ingalls) Grant, Oregon; cotton, pieced and appliqué, 73" x 83", Collection of Marjorie G. Colpitts, AQS 539p.*

Twenty-five "ultra-modernized" flower blocks designed by The Oregonian quilt columnist, C. Mullen, appear in this rare finished example. The startling use of black was deliberate and strongly recommended, and "if a bedroom was modernistic or exotic enough", all black blocks were deemed warranted.

Figure 2-35 *Ruth (Ingalls) Grant with her children Marjorie and Jay in Oregon, 1908. Courtesy Marjorie G. Colpitts.*

When the Grandmother's Flower Garden pattern was popular in the 1930s, Marjorie made her version she calls French Bouquet (*fig. 2.38*). During the ten years she taught school in Coos Bay, Oregon, she met with her sewing friends, "Las Amigas." At each session she would swap fabric and make a block for this quilt. Most of the hand quilting was done by Mrs. Cunningham, a neighbor. Marjorie considered this quilt her masterpiece and keeps it with all the other quilts made through the generations of her family. The quilts are carefully stored as textile testaments to the women and men who guided her and will continue to guide her family.

The link between hand-made objects and the people who make or own them is powerful. Unlike art objects which are viewed occasionally in a museum setting and become isolated from life or their original context, quilts made and used in the home remain integrated with life, bridging both past and present. Their reason for creation is not lost. Most traditional quilts were initially sewn for a utilitarian purpose, but just like so many other functional works of art, quilts served (and serve) other purposes as well. Through their fabric, design and color, quilts hold together pieces of experience and feeling which shape lives. The strongest memories are coupled with strong feelings, and these are often visual. They do not come in words but in colors and patterns. In some strong or subtle way, quilts are always expressive, always autobiographical. Even the most abstract of them are real, and revealing, serving to inspire and comfort.

Figure 2-37 *Marjorie G. Colpitts with a family quilt in 1998. AQS photograph by June E. Hall.*

Figure 2-38 *FRENCH BOUQUET detail, 1930-1940, Marjorie (Grant) Colpitts, Oregon; cotton, pattern pieced, 87" x 98", Collection of Marjorie G. Colpitts, AQS 538p. Marjorie considered this quilt to be her masterpiece.*

CHAPTER 3

FINDING THE TIME

Dana Fobes Bowne, Anne Caston, Elizabeth Shapland, and Mary Beth Smetzer

(above right) **Figure 3-1** *Women of the Matanuska Colony in Palmer hang clothes on the line. A Federal relocation program in the early 1930s brought "colonists" to farm in the area northwest of Anchorage. ASL PCA 270.645a*

(left) **Figure 3-2** *"Duck Neck" quilt detail, c.1905-1912, Jenny (Olson) Rasmuson. Yakutat, Alaska; preserved Alaskan species duck necks, pieced, 58" x 58", Collection of the Skagway Museum, #73-361, AQS 690sk. (Also see page 58.)*

IN 1910, ALASKA HAD JUST 64,356 PEOPLE; only 18,499 of these were women. Juneau, Sitka, and Fairbanks each had fewer than 4,000 in population, and Anchorage did not even exist. The gold rush days had doubled the territory's population of 1890, but by 1920 the decline of the gold rush led to a population decline in the territory and especially in the interior regions.[1] Even so, Anchorage grew quickly from its 1915 beginnings as a work camp for the building of the Alaska Railroad connecting Seward and Fairbanks,[2] and 1922 saw the start of classes at the land-grant institution in Fairbanks that became the University of Alaska in 1935.[3] The 1920 Census found the proportion of men to women less uneven, roughly 35,000 men to 20,000 women.[4] Life in the

Figure 3-3 *Jenny (Olson) Rasmuson (1880-1966). "She was definitely an Alaskan pioneer in the finest traditions of that term and adored by all who knew her." Courtesy of the Elmer E. Rasmuson family.*

Figure 3-4 *"Duck Neck" quilt, c.1905-1912, Jenny (Olson) Rasmuson, Yakutat, Alaska; preserved Alaskan species duck necks, pieced, 58" x 58", Collection of the Skagway Museum, #73-361, AQS 690sk. (See detail pp. 56-57.)*

cities of Alaska did not vary much from life in rural communities in the United States; many people enjoyed the modern conveniences of electricity, central heat, and telephones, though outhouses were still the norm. However, as today, life in the "bush" communities, with hunting, fishing, and gathering providing subsistence, was different from life in the cities.

A Subsistence Lifestyle

One of the most unusual made-in-Alaska quilts documented in the Alaska Quilt Survey resulted from subsistence activity; it was made of the iridescent necks of the ducks hunted by two missionaries in the central coastal Tlingit village of Yakutat *(fig. 3.4)*. Jenny Olson came to Yakutat in 1901 on missionary work for the Swedish Covenant Church. While there, she met Edward A. Rasmuson, a missionary as well as teacher and postmaster, whom she married in 1905. They had two children, Elmer and Evangeline. By living a subsistence lifestyle (both were "expert hunters"), they were able to save their salary and make a return visit to Sweden for three months in the summer of 1912. After the trip, the family moved to Minneapolis where they lived until their return north (to Juneau) in 1915.[5]

The "Duck Neck" quilt seems to be an "artistic consequence" of the subsistence economy on which the family lived while serving in Yakutat. Jenny noticed how beautiful the duck necks were and Elmer remembers his mother wanting to preserve those necks as beautiful objects in themselves and in memory of the family's times in Yakutat. And so she set out to make a quilt of the preserved necks of "Mallards, Canvasbacks, Pintails, Bluebills, Teals and others." Rasmuson says it took his mother a long time to make the quilt and that she preserved the skins by salting them and then sewed them together. She learned this procedure from the Tlingit Indians who followed it in making their ceremonial robes and ornaments for sale. She lined the skins with peppercorns to keep away any moths. The backing of the robe is made of old cloth which was sent from supporters of the mission in the states.[6] It appears Jenny used foundation piecing with muslin to support the skins. "Piece by piece, the artwork came alive."[7]

Such a creation might seem to be very fragile, but in fact another Alaskan source in the early 1950s suggested making parkas from the breasts of ducks, as such parkas are "warmer and more durable and cleanable than rabbit fur."[8] Even so, Elmer says that Jenny "kept the quilt folded and put away, occasionally bringing it out." Before her death in 1966, she donated the quilt to the Skagway Museum where it remains a "piece of the patchwork of Alaska history."[9]

Midwife in Seldovia

In one of the larger communities on the Kenai Peninsula, in the 1920s, Russian, Scandinavian, and Native women worked together to make wool and cotton quilts to be used by many in their town of Seldovia.[10] Florence (Bowen) Olssen Hammelbacher seems to have been the organizer of these activities. She was a midwife who not only assisted in about 375 births while in Seldovia but also housed many women from neighboring villages while they awaited their deliveries, encouraging them to quilt or crochet to pass the time. Florence Bowen was born in 1883 on Wood Island, near Kodiak, of Russian and Native descent. She attended the Russian and Russian-American School in Kodiak. By the time she was twelve years old, she was assisting a local doctor with his invalid wife. Soon, she began to assist him with other patients.[11] Florence had three husbands. She and her second husband, Charles Olssen, had ten children, five of whom survived into adulthood. Charles Olssen was Swedish and made dories. In 1912, after Mount Katmai erupted on the Alaska Peninsula some 600 miles distant from Kodiak, the family moved to Seldovia.[12] Her work with patients and people who had physical prob-

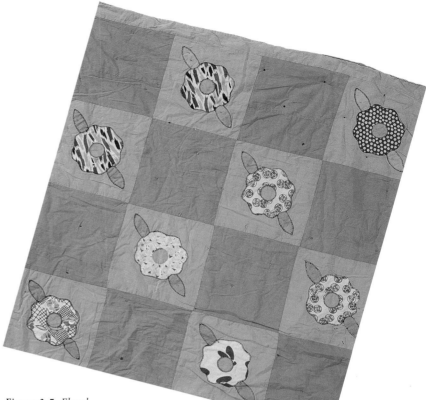

Figure 3-5 *Floral Appliqué detail, 1925-1940, Florence Olssen Hammelbacher, Seldovia, Alaska; cotton, appliqué, 64" x 82", Collection of Peggy Petersen Arness, AQS 1240ke.*

Figure 3-6 *Florence Olssen Hammelbacher in Seldovia holding a newly delivered baby and joined by family members. Courtesy of Mae Annette Fox Sharp.*

lems continued in Seldovia where she was also available as a translator for both Russian and Native languages.[13] Her third husband, Charles Hammelbacher, died in 1930,[14] at which time she left Seldovia for Seattle where she lived until her death in 1946.[15]

This kind and efficient woman was known for her quilts *(fig. 3.5)*, making them for family and friends. Though fabric was readily available in Seldovia, some of her quilts

Figure 3-7 *Textile handicraft display at the Matanuska Valley Fair in Palmer, c.1937. Photograph by Hewitts. Collection of John and Thelma Cope.*

incorporate flour sack material. Friends would pass on their fabric scraps to her for quilts. The batting was often wool and had to be ordered from the Neilson Sheep Ranch in Homer. She washed the wool and carded it herself. She made practical quilts for fishermen and fancier quilts for weddings. She even sold some.[16] But many were made by Florence for "her babies," the children she delivered. One of those births was little Peggy Petersen (Arness), whose actual delivery the midwife arrived too late to assist because Mr. Peterson had "stopped to talk" when sent to fetch the midwife. Despite her delay, Florence made a quilt for Peggy's birth and for her brother's birth as well.[17]

Fair Days
Many people today think of going to the fair to see quilts on display, and the same was true in the earliest days of Alaska's fairs. At the first annual Tanana Valley Fair, held in Fairbanks in September, 1924, an embroidered quilt made by a girls' club won a "special mention" award in the Boys and Girls Department.[18] From 1925 on, quilts merited a class or lot in every year's fair. Interestingly, from 1925 to 1927, "quilts" were a separate lot from appliquéd or embroidered "spreads," and then, in 1928, the categories were changed to three separate lots under Needlework: Quilting,

Patchwork, and Appliqué.[19] Organizers chose the same three categories for quilts for the Northwestern Alaska Fairs held in Nome in 1930 and 1931.[20]

Extension Service Help
By July 1930, when Alaska's population was almost back to the 1910 level,[21] homemakers in Alaska began to benefit from the activities of the Extension Service newly established at the college campus in Fairbanks. In her capacity as Assistant Director of Home Economics, Lydia Jacobson Fohn-Hansen was the first demonstration leader for the Extension Service, organizing nine 4-H clubs and twelve women's clubs in her first month of field trips.[22] In addition to publishing her "News Letter," she traveled all over the territory working with homemakers from 1930 to 1936 and then from 1940 to 1959. Her newsletters were full of information about food preparation, sewing, rug making, glovemaking, crocheting, and knitting. Fohn-Hansen was a skillful weaver[23] and wrote a great deal on the subject. Quilting was rarely mentioned. However, this may have been due to her focus on the skills a homemaker needed to feed and clothe her family or to provide income. It may or may not reflect the interest in quilting in the territory at that time. Fohn-Hansen described her work in a 1933 letter to Miss Ruth O'Brien, the Chief of the Division of Textiles and Clothing at the Bureau of Home Economics in Washington D.C. "During my last trip I gave quite a number of demonstrations on glovemaking.... We are using caribou and reindeer skins for the gloves and I am on the quest for information on home methods of tanning leather. Not all Alaskan homemakers are pioneers. Some in fact have all conveniences of modern city life but my work and my sympathy are with the people who are trying to establish homes under conditions which challenge all their abilities...."[24]

Fohn-Hansen did on a few occasions provide information about quilting in her newsletters, and the Homemakers' Clubs founded under the auspices of the Extension Service involved women in quilting activities to some extent. Apparently inspired by a quilt block she had seen in July 1932,[25] Fohn-Hansen published in the December, 1932 "News Letter to Homemakers," an article, "Showing How to Combine Pieces for Grandmother's Flower Garden Quilt," including a diagram of the flower unit and a template pattern. The reader was instructed to "cut out and trace on stiff paper to use as pattern," with suggested fabric colors of yellow for the centers, solid light green, solid cream or white and floral fabrics.[26] Though no sewing instructions were given, Fohn-Hansen reported in the next April's newsletter that since then she had seen quite a few Grandmother's Flower Garden quilts. "Pieced quilts are quite the vogue in Alaska, and many lovely ones are being made. The grandmother's flower garden is still a general favorite.... I believe the prettiest ones are set together with white or a row of white and a patch of green."[27] Alaskan quilters were staying in touch with quilting trends in the states. However, a search for quilt columns in Alaskan newspapers did not reveal any articles, unlike the many quilt columns that appeared in the "lower 48" papers.

Quilting may have been especially popular in the 1930s in Cordova, a community at the base of the Chugach Mountains on an inlet off the Gulf of Alaska. Cordova resident Florence Leahy O'Neill (1883-1959) made a Diamond Star quilt for her son, William, in 1932. She was born in Illinois and spent part of her childhood in Washington. Mrs. O'Neill attended a convent school where she perfected her hand sewing skills at a very young age. In 1908, she and her two young children traveled from Seattle to Cordova to join her husband, Harry O'Neill, who had arrived earlier. Ten more children were born in Cordova. In her large dining room, Mrs. O'Neill made quilts for family members, using a quilt frame set on the backs of the dining room chairs. Her daughter,

Florence O'Neill Imlach, remembers that friends of her mother came over to help her quilt. Fabric was obtainable by mail order or from a local seamstress who made dresses for the daughters. In 1937, when the O'Neills moved to Anchorage, Sears offered fabric for nine cents a yard.[28]

Fillings and Batts

Cordova was also Fohn-Hansen's source for advice she offered in her newsletter on acquiring cotton fillings for quilts from mail order companies. "The ladies of Cordova tell me that a pieced quilt to be used as a spread should be filled with 'China cotton' obtained from one of the favorite mail order houses. One pound will fill a quilt. For the quilting, some people think it easier to baste the quilt while on the frame, then remove it from the frame and do the quilting as you like."[29] But as early as 1916 both cotton and wool batts were available for purchase in Juneau, as were "silkolines and sateens in a good variety of patterns" for comforters. A Juneau newspaper advertised, "Just received big cotton batts, in a good quality cotton, also a pure wool Fleece in the regular comforter size, two pounds to the roll, much warmer and lighter than cotton."[30]

Figure 3-8 *Eskimo Brand flour sack, 1930s. Collection of June E. Hall.*

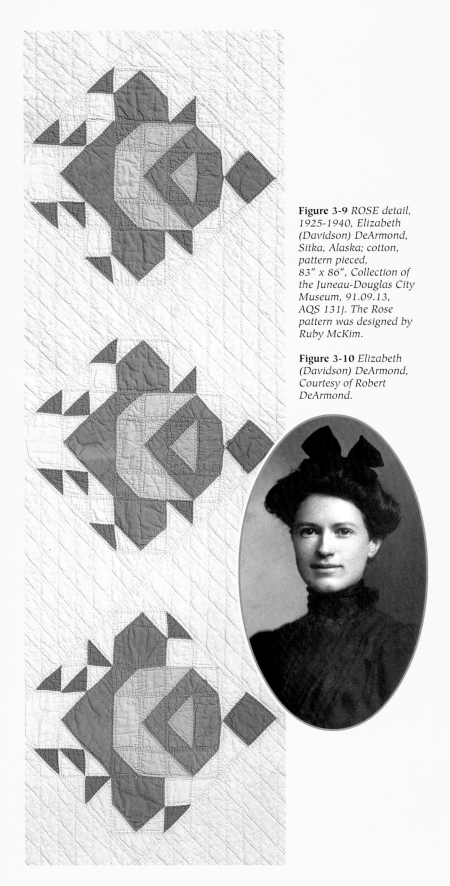

Figure 3-9 *ROSE detail, 1925-1940, Elizabeth (Davidson) DeArmond, Sitka, Alaska; cotton, pattern pieced, 83" x 86", Collection of the Juneau-Douglas City Museum, 91.09.13, AQS 131j. The Rose pattern was designed by Ruby McKim.*

Figure 3-10 *Elizabeth (Davidson) DeArmond, Courtesy of Robert DeArmond.*

Fohn-Hansen extolled these same attributes of wool, and she used her newsletter to promote local industries. "Every bed in Alaska should have good wool-filled quilts or blankets."[31] "Comforters should be filled with wool, as it is much lighter and warmer than cotton. Quilt fillings of good muslin, filled with virgin wool, home carded, may be purchased from farmers at Point Agassiz [near Petersburg in the Inside Passage]. Mrs. C. A. Swanson and Mrs. Andreas Ask will fill orders at reasonable prices."[32] "The women of Point Agassiz use an old country method… for carding wool…. It is especially nice for quilt and mattress fillings."[33]

Resurgence

The U. S. quilting revival that began in the 1920s and reached its crescendo in the late 1930s seems to have been paralleled in Alaska. One Alaskan woman was ambitious enough to enter a national quilting contest in 1934 and took away the prize for the entrant from the farthest distance. Minnie J. Wyly, a government school teacher at Ouzinkie on tiny Spruce Island northeast of Kodiak, had her quilt displayed in a huge three-day show which drew thousands of people in Detroit. Perhaps she was motivated by the $100 grand prize.[34] The winning quilt *(figure 2.29)* is shown on page 49.

Another Alaskan-made quilt of that era is the Ruby McKim Rose pattern quilt *(fig. 3.9)* which was made by Elizabeth (Davidson) DeArmond and is now in the Juneau-Douglas City Museum. Elizabeth, born in 1879 in Wisconsin, was a schoolteacher in Sitka from 1907 until she married; she then worked as a postmistress. According to Elizabeth's son, Robert N. DeArmond, his mother quilted for enjoyment, and she did far more weaving for garments, tablecloths, and scarves.

Matanuska Valley Colony

In May of 1935, 201 families from the northern counties of Michigan, Minnesota, and Wisconsin arrived as colonists to establish a farming community north of Anchorage in the relatively unpopulated Matanuska Valley, one of many government resettlement programs of the New Deal era.[35] The Extension Service was there to help them. Fohn-Hansen herself set up head-quarters in a tent and sold items the women had handcrafted, such as scarves, gloves in imitation pigskin, rag rugs, souvenir purses, knitting needles, and hot dish mats made of Alaska grass.[36] Fabric and notions were hard to come by, though a sewing machine was avail-able at a place called the Art Shop.[37] Neverthe-less, by 1938 the women of the valley were finding time for quilting, as evidenced at the Matanuska Valley Fair of 1938. The four classes for quilt entries were Embroidered, Patchwork, Appliqué, and Miscellaneous.[38]

These women may have brought their quilting skills with them from the states as did another Alaskan quilter, Lillie Darlin. Of Danish heritage, Lillie was born in Seattle in 1889 and began making quilts while living in Tumwater, Washington in the 1930s. She made her way to Alaska in 1938, and by the next year she was operating two inns in Sitka. Ten years later she helped her family run a lodge on the Alaska Highway. A prolific quilter, she sometimes bought stacks of machine-cut pieces of fabric in all shapes, sizes, and prints from a dressmaking company in the southeast that charged by the pound. Her Orange Peel quilt top *(fig. 3.12)* is typical of her hand-piecing skill. Her Trip Around The World quilt survived an apartment fire in Sitka in the early 1940s because it was in a metal trunk; its subsequent smoke marks are still visible. Her preference was for wool filler for a quilt as she liked the way it puffed up the quilting. She went to the additional work of preparing the wool herself, buying wool fleeces that had been washed, carding them herself, and saving up the carded wool until she had enough for a quilt.

Quilting continued throughout the 1930s as the territory's population grew, reaching 72,524 by 1939.[39] In Skagway in 1936, Jennie (Austin) Hahn, born in 1875 in Seattle, made a

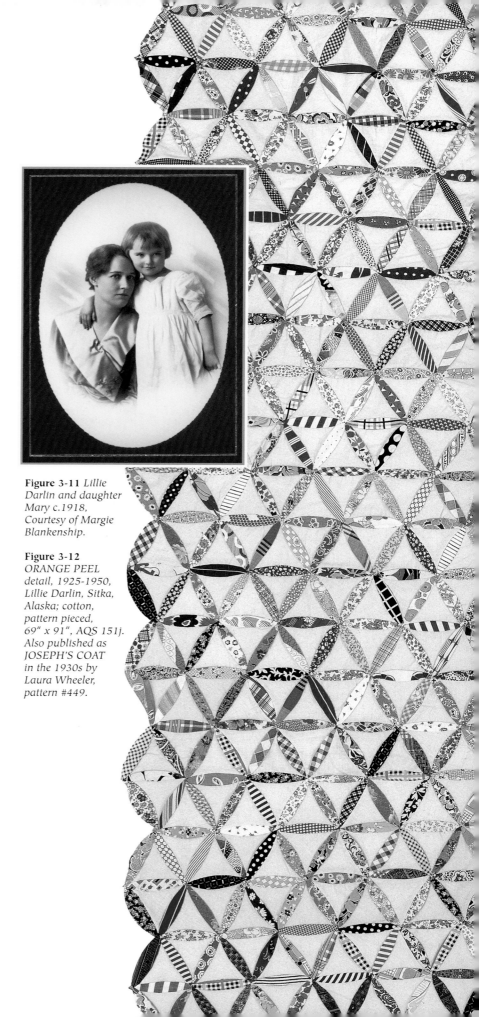

Figure 3-11 *Lillie Darlin and daughter Mary c.1918, Courtesy of Margie Blankenship.*

Figure 3-12 *ORANGE PEEL detail, 1925-1950, Lillie Darlin, Sitka, Alaska; cotton, pattern pieced, 69" x 91", AQS 151j. Also published as JOSEPH'S COAT in the 1930s by Laura Wheeler, pattern #449.*

Figure 3-13 *Pennant quilt, dated and signed "Feb. 1936, JAH," Jennie (Austin) Hahn, Skagway, Alaska; wool felt pennants, irregular pieced, 69" x 86", Collection of Karl Austin Hahn, Jr., AQS 961a. Jennie's creative nature led her to charcoal drawing, photography, collecting and pressing Alaskan wildflowers.*

Figure 3-14 *"Alaskan Memories" photographic album. Jennie Hahn recorded the boom town of Skagway and the building of the White Pass Railroad into Canada during 1898-1900. She developed the cyanotypes in her home darkroom. Collection of Karl Austin Hahn, Jr.*

Figure 3-15 *Alaska quiltmakers and their families about 1940. Left to right: Venetia E. Hahn, Karl A. Hahn, Sr., Venetia (Fehr) Pugh Reed, Jennie Hahn, Karl A. Hahn, Jr. (child) and Victor I. Hahn. Courtesy of Karl Austin Hahn, Jr. See Chapter 1 for the story of the quiltmaker, Venetia (Fehr) Pugh Reed.*

pennant quilt *(fig. 3.13)*. She moved to Skagway around 1898 and married Karl Hahn who surveyed for the White Pass Railroad and was superintendent of rails for 47 years. Under what circumstances she collected the various college and city pennants that make up the quilt is unknown.

A Moment in Time

The Sailboats quilt *(fig. 3.17)* is evidence of how lengthy the process of quiltmaking can be. Carol (Beery) Davis, born in 1890 in Ohio, moved to Juneau where she used her skill as a pianist to her advantage. She loved the barter system and exchanged piano lessons for dresses from a neighboring seamstress. Her daughter Connie says her mother made quilts for enjoyment, and that this particular quilt was a way "to catch a moment in time when her friends came and went." The dresses were exchanged for piano lessons in the 1930s and 1940s; Carol pieced the sailboats from the dress scrap fabric and had friends autograph them as she could catch them to do so. Though the quilt is, in a sense, a "friendship quilt," it appears not to have been a collaborative effort; rather, Carol made the quilt herself and had friends sign the squares later. Carol's daughter says that the squares were pieced in the early 1940s, but that the quilt itself wasn't assembled until the 1970s. Because of the signatures of friends and acquaintances, and because she had deeply loved those friends who had signed blocks and moved on or died, Carol Davis passed the quilt down to her daughter after enjoying the quilt for a long time; she lived to the age of 99.[40]

The War Effort

During World War II, quilting in Alaska as elsewhere seems to have been utilitarian in focus. Fohn-Hansen's newsletter of April, 1942 advised homemakers to "Store winter clothing

Figure 3-16 *On the docks of downtown Juneau, Carol (Beery) Davis (middle) poses with musicians Edythe Rowe and Matilda Holst (from left) and her daughters, Sylvia, Connie and Shirley. Trevor Davis photograph. Courtesy of Connie Davis.*

Figure 3-17 *SAILBOAT detail, 1930-1950 (finished in 1970s), Carol (Beery) Davis, Juneau, Alaska; cotton and synthetics, pattern pieced, 70" x 100", Collection of Connie Davis, AQS 176j.*

Figure 3-18 *HEXAGON child's quilt, c.1944, Lillie Darlin, Sitka, Alaska; cotton, pattern pieced, 27" x 41", Collection of Margie Blankenship, AQS 349s.*

During the war years, women in Juneau formed sewing groups under the auspices of the Red Cross to help clothe the world's children. At first there was no central workroom and "the work was done in individual homes, by church groups, lodge groups and other community groups." Together these women made 6,500 garments for what were called "Toddler Packs" and also layettes that included quilts and blankets. Frugality was the rule in such efforts, and as so often is the case, that led to quiltmaking. "Everything in our work room is made use of. Nothing is wasted. Baby quilts and lap robes for wheel chair patients have been made from the scraps left over from various garments." There was work for all. "Perhaps some shut-in wants a part — someone who can neither sew nor knit. There is much material to be cut into quilt pieces...."[42]

Baby Boom

When the war was over in 1945, women returned to less utilitarian quilting. As a Christmas present for her granddaughter, Lillie Darlin, who had moved to Juneau, made a doll quilt of hexagon prints in 1940s colors *(fig. 3.18)*. And with the baby boom came baby quilts. Josephine Hodgins of Sitka made a satin baby quilt *(fig. 3.20)* for a child who would think of Josephine forever as her grandmother though in fact they were not related. Josephine was born in North Carolina and made her way, along with her sister Lydia, from North Carolina to Alaska in the early 1900s where they both worked as teachers. "Jo" married the local dentist, Dr. Harry Hodgins, and they lived in Sitka until about 1964 or 1965. The Hodginses met Charles W. Kidd of West Virginia, who was stationed on nearby Japonski Island in the early years of World War II. A local tradition encouraged residents to invite servicemen into

safely — there will be no new wool for civilian use, so take care of what you have.... In sorting old clothing, thrift demands that everything be saved and sorted so as to be put to some good use. From socks, make mittens; from wool that cannot be remodeled into clothing, make quilts or rugs; from old cotton, make dress protectors, aprons, quilt protectors, mattress pads, dust cloths, carpet rags, and all kinds of rugs." She also refers to the possibility of recarding "an old wool quilt," stating that a three-pound batt requires about five pounds of raw wool.[41]

their homes for holidays and bridge. Later, after Charles Kidd was wounded in Europe, the Hodginses invited him and his wife to move to Sitka from West Virginia. Sitka needed young people, and the Hodginses had become attached to him. The Kidds' daughter Maryjo, who was named Mary after her mother and Josephine after Mrs. Hodgins, was born in 1945, and Jo made this quilt for her. Maryjo's family represents two aspects of the growth of Alaska in the 1940s: an influx of adults and the baby boom. The 1950 census showed a population (128,643) more than double that of two decades before.[43]

Thrift Division

Fairs were suspended during World War II, but when they started up again in 1947, quilts were again included with Patchwork and Plain lots. All along, the Tanana Valley Fair had awarded prizes only to "bonafide residents" of the Territory of Alaska, and in 1948 called for entries to the Textiles and Clothing Division. The superintendents reiterated the distinction between quilts made in Alaska ("homemade quilts") and those from the "old country," asking for both to be entered for display, but noting that only the Alaskan-made quilts would be eligible for prizes.[44] In the Matanuska Valley, a Thrift Division existed at the fairs at least by 1947, including a class for "Articles made from flour, sugar or grain sacks," with a lot for bed linen. The 4-H Club Work Division included a Home Improvement class with a lot for "Bedding and Bedspread, quilt, sheets, pillowcases, etc." Pieced quilts made of silk or rayon had their own lot in the Matanuska Valley fairs in 1955-58, perhaps a response to quilts being made of the latest dressmaking scraps.[45]

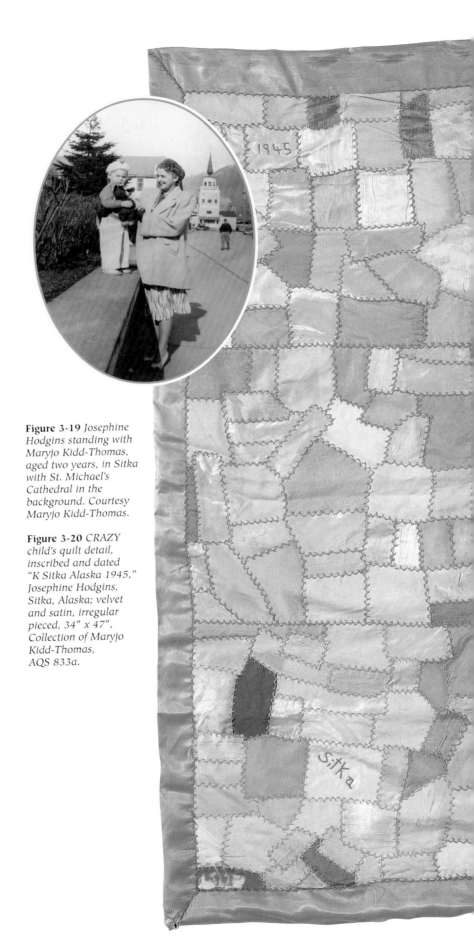

Figure 3-19 *Josephine Hodgins standing with Maryjo Kidd-Thomas, aged two years, in Sitka with St. Michael's Cathedral in the background. Courtesy Maryjo Kidd-Thomas.*

Figure 3-20 *CRAZY child's quilt detail, inscribed and dated "K Sitka Alaska 1945," Josephine Hodgins, Sitka, Alaska; velvet and satin, irregular pieced, 34" x 47", Collection of Maryjo Kidd-Thomas, AQS 833a.*

The Homemakers' Clubs continued to be involved with quilting in the 1950s, while the territory's population soared to well over 200,000 people at statehood with around 43 per cent women.[46] In 1955, "There were 1,299 women enrolled in Alaskan home demonstration clubs, 350 more than in 1953...."[47] In this way the Extension Service touched many women's lives. Extension newsletters reporting on one club's quilting project may have given the idea to quilt to other clubs. In 1954, the Big Delta Homemakers planned "quilt making" as one of their projects for the coming year.[48] The Ninilchik Homemakers' Club, organized in January of 1954, made a quilt for the Ninilchik Community Fair held in September, 1954.[49] The Alaska Homemakers' Council surveyed Homemakers' Clubs in the territory in 1955 and reported that "one club revived the art of quilting."[50]

Good Causes

Clubs began to realize the potential of quilts for raising money for good causes. The Northend Homemakers' Club of Ketchikan reported in 1958, "This year we completed and have or will raffle off by fall a braided rug and a homemade quilt. By these sales we have been able to contribute $25 to each of the following charities: Alaska Crippled Children, Building Fund for the Children's Home, Basket for a Needy Family, Cancer Fund, and to Polio Fund."[51] A 1953 newsletter reported that the Moose Pass Homemakers' Club devoted that year's programming to Handicrafts, and its twenty members "quilted a handmade quilt which was raffled for the benefit of the Community Library building fund."[52] Quilter Gladys "Happy" Sherwood was active in the Juneau's Mendenhall Homemakers during the 1950s and her group annually made a quilt to be raffled.[53]

Extension Service records also included details of some very early "wearable art" in the May, 1958 newsletter of the Matanuska Valley Homemakers. "Friendship Skirts, the newest

Figure 3-21 *Gladys "Happy" Sherwood, a member of the Mendenhall Homemakers (Juneau), quilted at her dairy farm and her group raffled a quilt every year during the 1950s for charity fund raising. Curtis Sherwood photograph. ASL PCA 150.85.*

idea about town, are being modeled by Myrtle Graham and Vivian Goodrich. They look like crazy patchwork quilts made into skirts — and that's just what they are. The girls say to take the pattern of your favorite flare skirt (not too full) and cut a foundation. Then collect scraps of material from all your friends and appliqué them on the foundation skirt in crazy quilt style. Makes a very attractive garment."[54]

It is easy to assume that the demands on Alaskan women to keep themselves, their families, and others in their communities well prepared for life in the north kept them too busy to pursue aesthetic interests, but the histories of women's clubs throughout the territory show continual interest in art and hobby shows, talks on needlecrafts, and fair exhibits.[55] As costly as travel to the states was, many people did make frequent trips "outside" to visit family and friends and thus stayed connected with cultural trends in the states. Quilting fluctuated in popularity in the years 1910-1959 in Alaska just as it did in the states, but all along some women continued to find comfort, enjoyment, and artistic expression in the art of quilting.

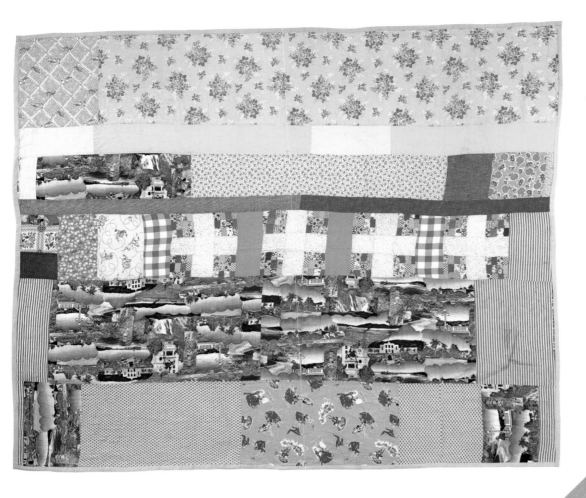

Figure 3-22 *STRIP, c.1950s, Marge Ware, Nikiski, Alaska; cotton, irregular pieced, 73" x 86", Collection of Lavonne Currier, AQS 1207ke. Originally from Milan, Missouri farm country, Marge made her way to Alaska and homesteaded with her husband on the Kenai Peninsula. An organic garden and chickens kept her busy, but if she could get her husband "to do the dishes and clean the house, she could make her quilts a lot faster." For her, quilts don't "take on a personality until they are quilted."*

Figure 3-23 *DRESDEN PLATE detail, c.1955, Harriet E. (Dearing) McIlree, Anchorage, Alaska; cotton, pattern pieced, 79" x 95", Collection of Elizabeth Huey, AQS 1222ke.*

Figure 3-24 *Quilt label on the back of figure 3-22 showing photograph of Harriet E. (Dearing) McIlree. "Hattie" was born in Pike County, Indiana in 1894 and made this quilt many years later for her Alaskan home. Collection of Elizabeth Huey.*

CHAPTER 4

SHARING A TRADITION

THE MANY ESKIMO, ALEUT, AND INDIAN GROUPS that occupy Alaska had extensive sewing traditions of their own previous to contact with "outside" cultures. The American quiltmaking tradition crossed cultural lines into these long established indigenous societies sometime in the nineteenth century. However, out of the over 1,500 quilts documented during the Alaska Quilt Survey, only one Native quilt made before 1959 was registered. Due to time and financial constraints, the survey was able to conduct only limited searches for more non-Western made quilts. Therefore, included in this chapter are a brief essay on Tlingit quilts and a reprint of the Ann Fienup-Riordan essay on Yupik quiltmaking from the book, *To Honor and Comfort: Native Quilting Traditions*.

(above left) **Figure 4-1** *Chief Shake's Hou Fort Wrangel, Alaska. Clan items are hel children and also sit on the patchwork qu spread out in front of the door. Winter an Pond photographers, ASL PCA 87.117.*

(right) **Figure 4-2** *RAVEN DESIGN, c.19 Margaret Ikenberry, Beatrice and Arnold Seattle, Washington; synthetic blends, pa pieced, 72" x 84", Collection of Cecilia K AQS 182j. At Tlingit memorial potlatches, hosting clan thanks the opposite clan for support by distributing gifts. This quilt, m by members of the Eagle clan, was given t Cecilia Kunz, an elder of the Raven clan, potlatch for Elizabeth Edwards of Dougla Cecilia remembers strips of cloth also bein given away at earlier potlatches.*

Figure 4-3 *Takou Chief Lying in State, Alaska. Prominently displayed with other clan ceremonial art of the deceased is a simple triangle pieced quilt. The body is covered with a button blanket. Winter and Pond photographers, ASL PCA 87.268.*

TLINGIT QUILTS

Peter L. Corey

THE REPERTOIRE OF TLINGIT INDIAN woven textile technology is extensive and includes Raven's Tail and Chilkat weaving techniques as well as twined spruce root and plated cedar bark basketry. Traditionally, Native Tlingits used sewing methods also found in Western quiltmaking. Actual quilting, layers of materials joined by sewing, was done by the Tlingit on some hide armor where layers, usually two, of thick hide were super-imposed and tied or sewn in place. Pieced construction was practiced in Tlingit culture prior to actual formalized Western quilting instruction. Different leather, fur, and bird skin pieces were sewn together in a geometric, patchwork style, usually to form small bags. Women of high status wore pieced skin robes of marmot or ground squirrel.

Appliqué is handsomely demonstrated in Tlingit ceremonial robes commonly referred to as button blankets that appeared in Southeast Alaska sometime in the mid-nineteenth century. These unquilted robes were made from wool trade blankets or trade cloth, usually dark blue or black, bordered on three sides in red with a large appliqué of totemic art sewn in the center. The edges of the border and the appliqué were covered or outlined with hundreds of mother of pearl buttons obtained in trade.

Native women began sewing with metal needles and commercial thread when woven textiles were introduced by the Euro-Americans. As early as 1832, Russian Kryill Khlebnikov wrote, "…on [sic] Sitka they want to have clothes made not of regular soldier's cloth but from good frieze or fine wool."[1] Tlingit women made use of a variety of commercial cloth, including calico[2] which, according to Khlebnikov, was "used mainly in Sitkha [sic] for trade with the Kolosh [Tlingit], who are paid in calico for small for [sic] pelts."[3] When Lady Franklin and her niece, Sophia Cracroft, visited Sitka in 1870, Sophia noted in her diary, "We saw some [Tlingit women] sewing, upon a dry patch outside their house; one was making a sort of garibaldi [blouse] very neatly — it was made of pieces of various patterns & colors sewn together into the right shape."[4] Other writings of the time suggest that the Native choices of color and design patterns did not match the standards considered acceptable or proper by Victorian women of the period.

With Russian colonization and the later American missionary efforts, schools became a part of Tlingit life. American style domestic arts were a large part of the school girls' education; sewing and other needlework were emphasized. In 1883, Mrs. Caroline Willard, a missionary to Haines, wrote that she taught the girls "to cut and fit their own clothing and they have learned to sew on the [sewing] machine better than most girls of their own age at home."[5] An 1895 missionary newsletter observed that Native girls were sewing quilt pieces at the Presbyterian Mission's Training School in Sitka.[6] Therefore, we can assume that quilting was taught along with other needlecrafts to the Indian girls attending schools in Southeast Alaska.

Early Tlingit quilts are few in number, and the Alaska Quilt Survey registered only one. The simple Bricks pattern quilt was made in Sitka around 1900, and it was sewn from a suit salesman's woolen samples. Emma Widmark offered the observation that most early Tlingit quilts were considered utilitarian bedcovers and thus did not survive daily use. When Emma was a girl in Klawock, she slept under a Crazy quilt until it was worn out. Tlingit women at the turn of nineteenth century made quilts, but later generations were drawn to other types of fine needlework like crocheting.[7] Anna Katzeek, originally from Klukwan, made a utilitarian quilt for her young son in the 1940s. Unfortunately, the quilt was destroyed in a 1947 house fire. In the early twentieth century when Cecilia Kunz was a young girl in Juneau, she helped her mother make quilts by hand-cranking the small sewing machine her mother used. Through the years, Cecilia and other Tlingit ladies made quilts that were given away at memorial or commemorative events such as the one in figure 4.2. Cecilia said the quilts were considered important gifts.[8]

The limited nineteenth century photographic record showing Tlingit people and quilts is inconclusive. All the quilts in the photographs are pieced examples with large squares and simple designs made from solid and patterned fabrics. These quilts might have been Native-made or possibly given as gifts or traded to the Natives. The photograph, "Takou Chief Lying in State, Alaska" (fig. 4.3), raises an interesting question. Shown in the photograph, along with the Yanyeidi clan's "Raven Capturing the Sun" headdress and the "Wolf" hat and other at'oow, is a piecework quilt prominently displayed in the lower left-hand corner. At'oow among the Tlingit are clan-owned treasures associated with songs, dances, and oral traditions that represent aspects of the clan's history and kinship. As in this photograph, at'oow were displayed at significant times and events such as potlatches. Is the quilt's appearance in this photograph by happenstance, or is it purposely placed as a treasured clan object?

At'oow in Tlingit culture serve to express and preserve clan identity. Quilts in American society have become objects of great reverence within families; they speak to family solidarity; separations were softened when heirloom quilts were taken as remembrances of times, people, and places past. Over time, certain quilts became a part of a family's oral and written tradition, a link to the past and a textile album for the future. Perhaps, the treasured quilts are a non-Native form of at'oow.

Figure 4-4 *Canopied with bolts of calico, Tlingit canoes loaded with dancers come to shore at Sitka for a berry feast in 1889. This annual memorial potlatch incorporated a distribution of gifts including the calico from the canoes, and from the calico-decorated houses on shore. The fabric was torn into strips of one to two yards and given away along with blankets and berries. George T. Emmons photograph, Royal British Columbia Museum PN1580.*

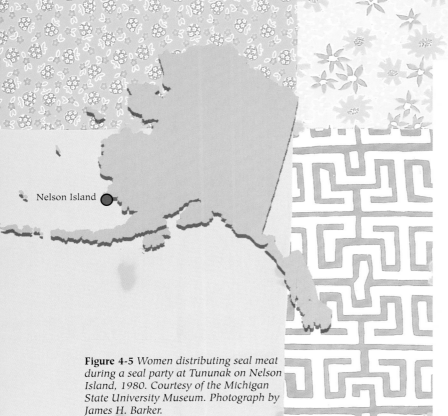

Figure 4-5 *Women distributing seal meat during a seal party at Tununak on Nelson Island, 1980. Courtesy of the Michigan State University Museum. Photograph by James H. Barker.*

NELSON ISLAND sits six hundred miles west of Anchorage, on the Bering Sea coast of Alaska. Today, close to two thousand Yupik Eskimos make their homes there, divided among five villages ranging in size from two to six hundred people. Each community supports a cash economy, and families have access to many aspect of Western technology, including television, snowmobiles, telephones, electricity, and, in some cases, running water. In many ways, though, these men and women still live a subsistence life comparable to that of their forebears. A primary occupation of Yupik men is fishing and sea mammal hunting, and women devote weeks to processing the catch. Yupik dancing and traditional ritual distributions remain important parts of community life. Although most young and middle-aged community members are bilingual, Yupik continues to be a child's first language and is the primary language of village residents over fifty.

Imagine a "typical" Eskimo family— peaceful hunter, wife, and child surviving on their own in an inhospitable homeland. This well-known stereotype, however, originated in the Central Canadian Arctic and does not apply to the Yupik Eskimos of Alaska, who are anything but typical. Far from merely surviving, their environment provides them with a wealth of resources, including seals, walrus, beluga whales, both oceangoing and freshwater fish, waterfowl, small mammals, moose, musk oxen, bears, berries, and greens. Although the low-lying coastal plain is treeless, every spring the rivers wash down an abundance of driftwood that the people traditionally used to build semisubterranean sod houses and elaborate ceremonial paraphernalia. Yupik families do not live in isolated igloos. Rather, during the winter ceremonial season people gather into communities running as large as three to four hundred residents.

"HOW YUPIK WOMEN SPOIL THEIR CLOTH"
The Seal Party Quilts of the Nelson Island Eskimos

Ann Fienup-Riordan

I ASKED A YUPIK FRIEND, Julia Nevak, to tell me what I should say about the colorful quilts found today in every home on Nelson Island. She smiled and said, "Tell them how Yup'ik women spoil their cloth!" I smiled back, remembering the first seal party I'd seen so many years ago and how surprised I was to see women tearing up whole bolts of cloth and throwing the pieces into the air as gifts to their neighbors. Even before I saw the colorful quilts they made from these strips, I was a convert.

I first came to the village of Toksook Bay on Nelson Island in May 1974, sent out from Anchorage to help with an economic development project. I soon found that the pottery project I had come to help with was in disarray. The people I spoke with, however, told me not to despair, that I had come at the best time of the year, that the seal parties were about to begin.

I'd never read about seal parties nor even heard of them. As I soon learned, seal parties were given when the men and boys of the village brought home their first bearded seals of the season. The festivities were full of excitement and lots of fun, as not only was the meat and blubber of every man's first-caught seal given away, but lots of other things were given away as well.

They began the next day — three parties in a row. I was just up and having a cup of tea when a little girl came to the door and said to come quick. There, right next door, a woman was standing on her porch throwing diapers and packs of gum into the waiting hands of a large group of women. She also threw strips of cotton cloth, which were carried by the wind in every direction. I joined the fun and followed the group to the next house for a repetition of the event, noticing that not all the same women attended and new women joined the

group. I asked about this later and was told that when a woman gives her seal party, her relatives could not attend; only nonrelatives received the gift of meat.

At the turn of the century, seal parties, or *uqiquq* (from *uqur*, which means oil or fat, lit-erally "one that is provided with oil"), were standard practice all along the Bering Sea coast of southwestern Alaska, and they are still common in many coastal communities today. With the introduction of trade goods in the early 1900s, crackers and a teaspoonful of tea were added to the distribution, growing to the elaborate disbursements of store goods that accompany the gift of seal meat on Nelson Island today.

The island women do not remember a time when they did not include strips of cloth in their seal parties. Cotton drilling and calicos were popular materials at the Tununak trading post from the 1800s on. In the 1940s, a woman could get twenty-five cents for a handwoven grass basket, enough to buy a yard of cloth. Women from fish camps on the southern side of the island would walk twenty miles over the

Figure 4-6
Women reaching for cloth thrown during a Toksook Bay seal party, 1977. Courtesy of Michigan State University Museum. Photograph by Ann Fienup-Riordan.

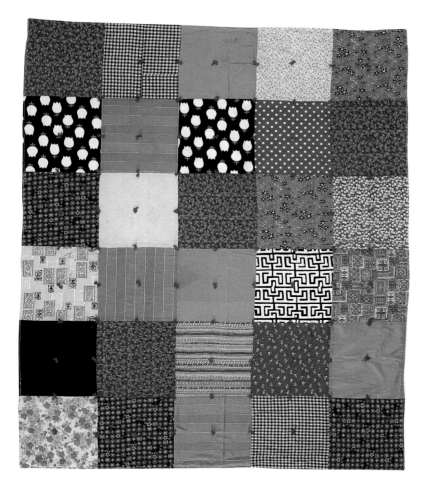

mountain and back to attend Mass in the Tununak church, bringing their baskets with them and taking home cloth, tea, and matches in return.

In preparation for a seal party on Nelson Island today, the seal is brought inside the house, placed on big pieces of cardboard on the floor, and cut across the stomach right down to the meat. The skin is removed together with the fat, and the fat is cut into strips two feet long and four inches wide, bordered on one side by a thick piece of skin. The women then cut the meat into pieces to pair with the fat.

After the seal is divided, the store-bought goods are also cut up, cloth strips are torn, string is cut, boxes of cookies and tea are opened, and packs of gum are undone. Then the party begins. Katie Moses described the seal party as she remembered it when she was little:

> *I'd run to invite ladies. All excited, they would jump and leave whatever they were*

doing, even hot tea. The seal party comes first. With good hunting they are continuous day after day. It is a belief that women celebrate the first mukluk [bearded seal] of the spring so their husbands and sons who catch their first seal will gain as successful hunters. It symbolizes the sharing of thankfulness. During the springtime, the village comes alive with living sounds. The bright sun beats down, reflecting on the white snow, blinding the people at the same time and tanning anybody who is enjoying the springtime. Rushing to the house where the husband caught a mukluk, you would think that the women are racing on the Fourth of July. Usually the women want to get the best position.[9]

The women gather outside the hostess's home. Everyone has either an enamel pan or a plastic or tin bucket, which they place at the porch entrance. The goods to be distributed come originally from the outside, the male domain, and enter the inside, the female domain, for preparation. Their distribution both extends and redefines relationships within the village, between men and women and between families, as raw seal meat (the new, harvested food) and canned tuna (the prepared, processed food) are temporarily juxtaposed and then one after the other thrown into the air.

When everyone is gathered, the porch door opens and the hostess begins to throw hunks of blubber into each bucket. The blubber is followed by the distribution of large chunks of meat, one piece for everyone, with the better parts as well as the leftovers given to older women. While men are excluded from the seal party, small children gather round hoping for edible tidbits. Later in the day, girls will play at diminutive seal partying, with shreds of cloth, bits of cracker, and pieces of rock.

Following the seal come pieces of salmon soaked in seal oil, dried fish, squares of sealskin leather, pieces of string or colored yarn measuring about five inches long (these will be tied to fish hooks as bait), *giluq* (strips of dried seal gut, twenty of which can be sewn together to make a waterproof parka), and strips of cotton cloth, as long as the width of a bolt and about six or seven inches wide.

But that is not all. Following these staples come, in no apparent order, candy and cigarettes, candy cigarettes, plastic beads, an occasional Frisbee, disposable diapers, needles, gum, bars of soap, apples, more strips of cloth, toilet paper, and Mexican hats. Soap powder and loose tea also are scooped from big boxes and given to the waiting women, who neatly hold out the hem of their loose fitting cotton dresses, pour in the powder or tea leaves, gather them into a knot and tie it tight with one of the pieces of string. There is laughter and mounting confusion as the giveaway gets going. Of everything given there is always too much, and the hostess throws the extra in the air in a random direction. Things keep hitting people in the head. I talked to one girl who had just given her first seal party. She said that the oldest women had advised her to close her eyes while the women tried to attract her attention with their "Me! Me!" gestures. Women snap things up quickly and pop them into the large front pockets of their dresses with a wonderful grace. When there is nothing left to throw, each woman picks up her bucket and walks home.

The seal party offered a wonderful window into how the women of Nelson Island still thought about and acted on their concept of what it means to be related. Even more exciting, I found the seal party not an isolated relic of traditional culture but rather part of an annual cycle of ritual distribution. Its immediate counterpart on Nelson Island is the men's and women's exchange dance (*kevgiruaq*), in which men and women are said to "fight through the dance."

On the first night of the exchange dance, all the women in the village pair up as married couples, one woman taking the part of the husband and the other the part of the wife. Then, together, the women dance a multitude

of gifts into the community hall and on the following morning give them out to the men of the village. The men perform for the women on the following evening, and the next morning the women receive their gifts in turn. The entire sequence of dances and gift-giving takes hours and hours, as everyone in the community has a turn on the dance floor. The particular dance performed is always the same, but each couple vies with the others to make its rendition particularly hilarious.

Even if one knows nothing about Yup'ik cultural configurations, the exchange dance is still a splendid and exuberant performance to behold. Seen in the light of the seal party, its eloquence is apparent. Whereas in the seal party gifts are thrown out the doors of individual houses, in the exchange dance gifts are danced in the door of the community hall. In the seal party, these gifts consist of strips of cloth and bits of string and bits and pieces of every conceivable household commodity. In the exchange dance, whole cloth and full skeins of yarn are given. In fact, many of the goods distributed during the midwinter dance contain, in abundance, the stuff of seal party gifts. Even the order in which the goods are given replicates the order of the seal party distributions. Nelson Islanders recognize this parallel, with some younger women voicing how this was one of the important things about dancing: "We get what we need for the spring, which is soon!"

After the dance, when the servers have finished the initial distribution of gifts of obviously equal value, such as twenty one-pound cans of Crisco, the floor is opened to choice. Each woman, going from eldest to youngest, has her pick of what remains. The first things chosen are the long, colorful pieces of cloth, from six to twenty feet in length and stretched out by the servers, as they were by the dancers when they were presented, so that everyone can admire their length and pattern.

As many goods leave the store and begin the cycle of reciprocity at the winter dance, others end their journey. Among the most valued are the quilts and bedspreads made of strips of cloth from seal parties gone by. Parents give these *ulit* (blankets) in the name of their children, and they are specifically directed to elders or honored guests.

The strips of cloth given at the seal party are a miniature of the bolt of cloth spread out for display during the dance, in part-for-whole relation to it. The patchwork quilt that reappears during the succeeding dance distribution is a qualitative transformation of the bolt. In the same way, the gut parkas worn by ocean hunters and by the shaman during spiritual hunting trips are constructed from strips of dried gut distributed in the seal parties. What is introduced into the exchange system — bolts of cloth, rolls of gut — during the winter dancing will be taken apart, cut and distributed for the spring seal party. Alternately, the articles that exit from the cycle during the winter distribution — such as quilts and rain parkas — are a fabrication from seal and seal party parts. Here seasonal and ritual cyclings are equated with movement between taking apart (cutting and tearing) and fabrication.

A woman routinely tears the length of cloth that she receives in the midwinter exchange dance into strips for her spring seal party distribution. With the strips of cloth that she herself has collected from the various seal parties, she fabricates a simple pieced cover to give away during the next year's exchange dance. If all that was required was a cover for the bed, the Yupik people have certainly taken a circuitous route to ensure its provision. Their worldview, their whole cultural mode of being, has been put on stage along with the dancers, acted out, and so reestablished and reaffirmed. Instead of a moral on the order of "never the twain shall meet," the Yupik celebrations seem to imply that which is separated (socially, physically, and, as we shall see, metaphysically) will in the end be reunited.

Although village elders are given the preferred position and choicest gifts in both the seal party and exchange dance distributions, the result is honor without wealth. The older women redistribute the gifts they receive within their families. Cloth and diapers go to their daughters and daughters-in-law (and ultimately to their grandchildren), and candy goes directly to the children.

Age is doubly honored. The older matrons are given as their due that which they will dispense with the magnanimity appropriate to their years. Thus, a social as well as biological and historical cycling is apparent. The goods exchanged between the women of different families are used to delineate the hierarchy of sharing among the women of each individual family. But the goods do not stop here. With circularity appropriate in a culture caught up in cycling, the seal party guests are given gifts not to be used in the recipients' own seal parties but redistributed in a different form through the winter gift-giving. Cloth given to the older women in the seal party thus re-emerges as a quilt in the midwinter dance, sewn together to celebrate the grandchildren. The goods recycle through time, reconstituting social ties and illustrating a dynamic structure of life or reproduction.

Let me relate several more experiences to show how this point of view pervades village life today. In spring 1978 I revisited Nelson Island while pregnant with my first child. My Yupik friends proceeded to teach me the elaborate set of dos and don'ts that still accompanies pregnancy and childbirth in the village. I was to sleep with my head toward the door. As soon as I got up every morning, I was to run outside as fast as I could. Only then might I come in, sit down, and drink tea. In fact, any time during the day that I left the house I was to do it quickly without stopping in the doorway. If I were to pause in my exiting, the baby was sure to get stuck during delivery.

This series of prescriptions draws an obvious parallel between the womb in which the unborn baby lives and the house in which the expectant mother resides. Analogically, the throwing of gifts out of the house through the doorway at the time of the seal party is comparable to their birth. Analogous relationships exist between the progress of the souls of the human dead and the return of gifts into the community hall at the time of the exchange dance. Imagery of birth and rebirth pervades the Yupik system of symbols and meanings— the finality of death everywhere averted in both action and ideal.

Another anecdote helps clarify this cultural framework. When I returned to Toksook Bay with my newborn daughter in the fall of 1978, she was immediately named. The older woman who had been my teacher while I lived on the island had a cousin who had drowned not three weeks before. No sooner had my daughter and I come into the village than she came to where we were staying and gave my daughter the name of her dead cousin. Then, in every house in which we visited, people would ask me what my daughter's name was. When I told them, they would laugh and say such things as, "Oh, he's come back a *kass'aq* [white person]!" or "He always did want to learn English!" or "To think now he has red hair!"

All this verbal play on the baby's name was a kind way of welcoming my daughter into their midst. But, equally important, these endearments were wonderfully explicit expressions of the belief that in the newborn child the soul of the recently dead is born again. In the Yupik world, no one ever finally passes out of existence. Rather, through the naming process, the essence of being human is passed on from one generation to the next.

The cycling of souls is especially important in light of the traditional belief that the souls of seals must be cared for by the successful hunter so that they, too, will be born again. Seals as well as other animals are believed to give themselves to humans voluntarily. Yupik people do not view this as a necessary response on the part of the seals but as an intentional act in which they willingly approach the good

Figure 4-8 *Boys presenting gifts at the exchange dance, including a folded Seal Party Quilt, Nelson Island, c.1978. Courtesy of Michigan State University Museum. Photograph by Ann Fienup-Riordan.*

hunter in the ritual of the hunt. When the seal is "killed," it does not die; rather, its *unguva* (life) retracts to its bladder, where it remains until returned to the sea the following season. In the past, during the annual Bladder Festival, Yupik hunters and their wives inflated and feasted on the bladders of seals and other animal guests. After they had properly hosted them, they pushed the bladders down through a hole in the ice so the souls of the seals might be born again.

Through these events the circle is complete. As do the seasons cycle, so do whole bolts and bits of cloth. Human and animal souls likewise are continually in motion. The birth of a baby is the rebirth of a member of its grandparental generation. The death of the seal means life to a village. The "spoiling of cloth" by Yupik women is both the end of the bolt and the beginning of a quilt, a gift valued many times over. The same people and the same seals have been on this earth from the beginning, continually cycling and recycling between birth and rebirth. Through this cosmological circuit, a life-celebrating system is put forward, a celebration of life each Nelson Island quilt embodies.

SNAKES AND STREAKS OF LIGHTNING

Debbie Manion

(above right) **Figure 5-1** *Lydia and Sylvanus Stoltzfus with their children about 1938. Courtesy of Hilda Stoltzfus.*

(left) **Figure 5-2** *FAN detail, 1907-1925, Lydia (Hartz) Stoltzfus, Pennsylvania, AQS 1163h. (Also see page 82.)*

THE QUILT DISCOVERY DAYS held at many locations around Alaska served as dynamic, kaleidoscopic quilt shows. As part of the documentation process, quilts were raised and lowered every couple of minutes on a frame that allowed an entire quilt to be photographed. Displayed vertically, more like a painting than a bed covering, quilts often revealed fabulous graphic effects not easily noticed when they were laid flat or folded. In some mysterious way, each quilt enjoyed a few moments of fame and admiration. During this process, and much later, when the steering committee agonized over the selections for this book and the exhibit, some quilts immediately leaped forward as spectacular examples of design or construction while others had that indefinable quality that just endeared them to us. Some of the "textile stars" are included in this chapter.

Figure 5-3 *FAN, 1907-1925, Lydia (Hartz) Stoltzfus, Pennsylvania; cotton, wool, silk, linen, pattern pieced, 81" x 82", Collection of Hilda Stoltzfus, AQS 1163h. (See pp 80-81.)*

(right) **Figure 5-4** *CRAZY, 1925-1950, Lydia (Hartz) Stoltzfus, Pennsylvania; cotton, wool, velvet, rayon, irregular pieced, 69" x 85", Collection of Hilda Stoltzfus, AQS 1164h.*

Wedding Dress Included

Although quiltmakers are known for using materials at hand, Lydia (Hartz) Stoltzfus pushed the limits by using wool, cotton, linen, silk, velvet, rayon, and flannel. Her two quilts registered in the survey are distinctive not only for fabric choice, but for design as well. Family folklore indicates that even a piece of her 1907 wedding dress was included in the Grandmother's Fan quilt *(fig. 5.3)*. The quilt capitalizes on the clear, mellow colors yielded by the wool fabrics in combination with other materials of various contents and textures. The varied backgrounds of the fans enliven the quilt and cause the viewer to examine the "weather" each individual sunrise fan implies.

Lydia (1882-1967) was a German Mennonite who was born in Morgantown, Pennsylvania. Lydia made the Fan quilt early in the twentieth century.[1] While some people might anticipate a predictable use of designs and materials in quilts made by a member of a conservative religious group, Lydia took a more eclectic approach in executing her ideas.

Figure 5-5 *POSTAGE STAMP, 1925-1950, Lydia Barge, Minnesota; cotton, pattern pieced, 87" x 107", Collection of Marilyn Holmes, AQS 175j. Photograph by Marilyn Holmes.*

The Crazy quilt *(fig. 5.4)* made by Lydia further testifies to her adventurous spirit in designing quilts. This quilt appears to be a hybrid of the wool utility quilt and the Victorian Crazy. Even so, Lydia's rectangular and irregularly shaped pieces are far more austere than those found in typical, lushly embroidered Crazy quilt blocks. Lydia's quilt is built on color, a large variation in the sizes of the pieces, and her choice of interesting, eccentric shapes. These departures from the norm lend a Cubist quality typical of some of Picasso's work. However, Lydia chose to contain this vivid composition with a calm, striped homespun border.

Tenacious and Industrious

The lovely Postage Stamp quilt *(fig. 5.5)*, with its striking lattice of red and yellow squares running through it, is inextricably linked to a solar eclipse and a family visit. When Marilyn Holmes was six, she visited her great aunt at the family farm in Minnesota, and was subsequently given this wonderful quilt. Prior to World War II, needlework was commonly enjoyed by farm women as an outlet for both creativity and socializing. Lydia Barge, "Great Aunt Liddie," the quiltmaker, excelled among her family of needleworkers. (Mamie Eisenhower was the recipient of a shawl Lydia crocheted; it was kept at the Eisenhower country home.)[2]

This Postage Stamp quilt is a tribute to the tenacity and industriousness of Lydia Barge and other women of the era who routinely took on challenges few would contemplate today. Such feats were accomplished magnificently. The quilt is made of close to five thousand pieces of postage stamp-sized fabric meticulously arranged and sewn together by hand. The artist used vibrant and intense colors to distinguish the centers of the squares, but then surrounded the centers with calmer, subtler squares that vary with each block. The lively red lattice squares frame each block joining to form a unifying element that beautifully defines and enlivens the quilt. Exemplary hand

Figure 5-6 *FAN detail, 1925-1950, Bessie (Beyer) McGranahan, Missouri; cotton, pattern pieced, 77" x 89", Collection of Budd and Paulette Simpson, AQS 81j.*

quilting completes the quilt and adds dimension to the surface. Hung on the wall, the quilt's myriad of tiny squares imparts a shimmering Pointillist quality.

The Last Straw

Many of the quilt artists of the late nineteenth and early twentieth centuries led rigorous lives of unanticipated adventure and hardship. It is all the more to their credit that they were able to produce masterpieces in their precious spare time. Bessie Florence (Beyer) McGranahan (1886-1979) lived on her father's trading post in Nebraska until the family home and store were destroyed by a tornado. This proved to be the last straw for her mother, who had lost two children to diphtheria on the frontier. Bessie and her family moved to Virginia, Texas, and Missouri, where she became postmistress in

Figure 5-7a-b *GRANDMOTHER'S FLOWER GARDEN detail, 1925-1950, unknown maker; cotton, pattern pieced, 64" x 83", Collection of Ann Leuenberger, AQS 1497pm.*

her father's store. In 1906 she married James McGranahan. She pieced quilts until she died at the age of 93 years.[3]

One of Bessie's fabric sources was an elite dress manufacturer in Kansas City, Nelly Don. A bag of scraps cost one dollar. The colorful Fan quilt *(fig. 5.6)* certainly may have been made from some of the Nelly Don scraps. The fans, made from solid fabrics alternating with lighter prints, give this commonly used pattern added depth and visual interest. The neutral sashing effectively encases the fans but lets the eye wander from one fan to the next.

Fruitful Inspiration

A great deal of thought, and sometimes humor, went into many quilt designs. A garage sale find in Palmer of a Grandmother's Flower Garden *(fig. 5.7)* with a perfect ring of "fussy-

cut" oranges was a delightful and amusing surprise many years later when the quilt appeared for a Discovery Day. The quilt clearly shows the lengths to which quilt artists went to personalize their works.

Another motif that was much cause for laughter was the peeled banana in the Fruit Basket appliqué quilt *(fig. 5.8)*. The banana was the fourteenth block of the Fruit Basket quilt designed by Ruby McKim. Patterns for the thirty-two blocks of appliquéd fruit were published one per week in newspapers around the country in 1932. The directions begin with "All the riot of color and charming variety of form that are found in nature's abundant fruits are captured and conventionalized for the making of the Fruit Basket Quilt."[4] The blocks included such exotics (for the time) as kumquats, quince, persimmons, and pomegranates. The appliquéd portions of the blocks were published full size, with instructions that they be traced using carbon paper and that a seam allowance be added. A smaller drawing of the finished block was included so the quilter had an idea of how the finished block was meant to look.

Mary Rose (Bright) St. Clair made the Fruit Basket quilt for her son, as a wedding gift about 1932 when the family moved to Oregon.[5] She chose an unusual light brown fabric for the background that effectively shows off the baskets of fruit. The inner border is a combination of colored triangles apparently of the same fabrics as the fruits. The random colors form an imaginative frame for the meticulously pieced fruits. The fine quality of the appliqué as well as the hand piecing and quilting testify to Mary St. Clair's talent as a needleworker.

Although the idea of quilts made from kits or published patterns may imply a paint-by-number approach to quiltmaking, some of the most striking quilts in the survey were kit quilts. In spite of prescribed patterns or colors, quiltmakers invariably personalized their

FRUIT BASKET QUILT
NO. 14 BANANAS

Figure 5-8 *FRUIT BASKET, 1932, Mary Rose (Bright)*
St. Clair, Oregon; cotton, applique, 66" x 87", Collection
of Nancy Seimears, AQS 679w. Mary Rose (1872-1959)
homesteaded with her family in Wyoming in 1884. She married
at age fourteen and made many quilts as she moved West.

Figure 5-9 *ENDLESS CHAIN, 1925-1950, Mrs. Bottemueller, Missouri; cotton, pattern pieced, 74" x 92", Collection of Michele Fehlings, AQS 488sk.*

quilts through color choices, embellishments, or exceptional handwork. Many of the kit quilts are evocative of the era in which they were made and have an appeal all their own.

Extremely Crazy

While some quilters enjoyed the published designs or kits, others seized an idea and exploited it. The random shapes of the pieces and the embroidered edges indicate the maker of the Crazy quilt *(fig. 5.10)* was influenced by others who made Crazy quilts at the end of the nineteenth century. However, the use of many intensely patterned, upholstery-type fabrics led to a fascinating tapestry of piecing unlike any others seen either during the survey or in publication. The quilt artist used a palette of linen, cotton, delaine, and silk prints. Although the weights of the materials and the scales of the prints vary considerably, the overall embroidery is the unifying element. The quilt's intriguing surface causes the eye to roam searching out the next interesting element. It must have made a wonderful map that stirred the imagination of the owner, who slept under it as a child. This sumptuous quilt exudes a sense of adventure that even one hundred years later inspires the wish to meet the creator.

The Watercolor Quilt

Fabric and design decisions converge in mysterious ways to produce the elusive appeal of what was dubbed the "Watercolor" quilt *(fig. 5.9)* made by a Mrs. Bottemueller, a Missouri housewife of German descent.[6] The quilt artist explored the subtle blending of patterned fabrics long before the "watercolor" quilt craze of the 1990s through her choice of unusual, soft, large scale prints. The quilt pattern name, Endless Chain, accurately describes the interconnected daisies that float on the print background. The flowers seem to advance or recede

Figure 5-10 *CRAZY detail, unknown maker, 1880-1900; cotton, silk, linen, irregular pieced, 76" x 96", Collection of Karyn Janssen, AQS 1277f.*

depending on the color and intensity of the background fabrics. The orange flower centers add a further layer of interest as they echo some of the background colors. The pale peach border allows the pieced center of the quilt to present itself. Despite being a 1940s quilt, it stands out from others of that era through the use of the large-scale background prints and color combinations unusual to that time period. This was one of those quilts that was unassuming at first glance, but was immediately appealing when raised to be photographed.

(opposite page) **Figure 5-12**
PINEAPPLE, 1865-1900, attributed to
Lucy (Rash) Catron, possibly Montana;
wool, pattern pieced, 72" x 83",
Collection of Cindy Merriam, AQS 771v.

Figure 5-11 LOG
CABIN, 1865-1900,
Lydia Lang,
Lavinia Lang,
Angie Lang,
possibly New
Hampshire or
Maine; cotton,
pattern pieced,
63" x 73",
Collection of
Kenneth and Sue
Lang, AQS 1476a.

Sunshine and Shadow

The Log Cabin design has held a prominent
place among quilters for some time. This Log
Cabin quilt (fig. 5.11) was hand-pieced sometime between 1865 and 1900 by the owner's
great-great aunts Lydia, Lavina, and Angie
Lang. It was brought to Alaska from New
Hampshire as a family heirloom.[7] The reds and
greens are typical of the colors used in the
latter half of the 1800s; the colors reflect the
dye technology available at the time.

Log Cabin quilts are often studies in
contrasts and can present wonderful dimen-
sional illusions. Even though the Lang quilt
seems to have been made from scrap materials, the sisters artfully chose fabric colors and
prints to create a visual richness. The dark and
light strips of the "logs" have been sewn to
form positive and negative diagonal halves of
the blocks. The blocks have been set in the
Sunshine and Shadow configuration so that
the light and dark corners converge to form
larger areas of contrast. The quilt artists were
careful to alternate values even within the light
and dark areas, creating stripes that make this
quilt an exceptionally lively example of the
traditional pattern. The eye seeks the bits of
printed fabric among the dark strips that are a
busy contrast to the soft, sedate grays and off-
whites that tend to form a lattice on which the
heavier, darker blocks hang. The red center
squares have remained vivid and, at times,
seem to rise up off the surface of the quilt. In
the hands of inventive artists, this well loved
design becomes a curious combination of
homeyness and sophistication.

Electric Pineapple

The wool Pineapple quilt (fig. 5.12) is a real
visual treat. From the moment it was raised to
be photographed, the quilt inspired admiration
and envy at the Discovery Day in Valdez. Lucy
(Rash) Catron is believed to have made it
around the turn of the nineteenth century.[8] The
quilt has an advantage because it is made of
wool, which has the distinct ability to absorb,
retain and reflect intense color. The vibrant red
and red-orange "pineapples" appear to be
elevated from the background of navy, black,
purple, and gray. While at times a distinct
center square appears, others blend into the
background adding to the impression of floating
"pineapples." The light gray areas are a stark
contrast to the dark ground while the medium
gray and purples form ghost images beneath
the red foreground. The red ties used to attach
the layers appear and disappear like fireflies
looking for a place to land. One of the most
intriguing uses of fabric is the addition of a
tropical print to one end of an already spectacular quilt. The tropical print serves as a
removable chin protector to preserve the fabric
edge of the quilt and to keep the quilt clean.
This bold use of a completely incompatible
fabric for the chin protector is a peculiar delight.

Figure 5-13 *Kenton family quilters left to right: Lois Jones, Alice Haxton, Naomi Motz, with their mother Una Kenton, La Jara, Colorado,1930s. Courtesy of Larry and Lynette L. Motz.*

Figure 5-14 *"Chief Snake" Quilt, 1935, Naomi (Kenton) Motz, La Jara, Colorado; cotton, pattern pieced, 73" x 91", Collection of Larry and Lynette L. Motz, AQS 899a.*

The Chief Snake Quilt

The "Chief Snake" quilt *(fig. 5.13)* is one of the textile treasures in a long legacy of the Kenton family quilters. Una (Mount) Kenton learned to quilt from her mother and grandmother who lived in Tennessee. She subsequently shared her love of quilting with her daughters Naomi, Lois, and Alice. Many quilts, including the "Chief Snake" quilt, were made on the Kenton family farm in La Jara, Colorado. After Lois and Alice married, and Lois visited from Fort Collins, Colorado, and Alice from Gotebo, Oklahoma, quilting was a part of the festivities. Many envelopes went through the mail carrying messages and scraps of material that the sisters and their mother had saved for each other. They also exchanged hints on how certain patterns worked and ideas for future projects. The sisters remained close, and at the ages of 98, 95, and 92 were still sharing in each other's lives.[9]

Naomi (Kenton) Motz was 29 years old when she made the "Chief Snake" quilt for her son, Larry Motz when he was born in 1935. After Naomi married, she lived near her mother in Alamosa, Colorado. Together they went to a friend's house in Del Monte where her mother acquired the pattern. The regional name of the quilt reflects its western origins; the pattern is elsewhere referred to as New York Beauty. Family history relates that the quilt is named for an Indian chief who was a member of one of the tribes that inhabited Indian Territory, now the state of Oklahoma. The color scheme is also linked to Native American history. Yellow symbolizes the sun, red — fire, and green — grass. The white and red quarter circles represent "pale and red faces;" the serrated borders of the circles are like the turkey feathers of the headdress; the green swastikas are good luck symbols. Three thousand pieces converge to form several different patterns. The colors used in this quilt provide a western flavor quite distinct from a more traditional rendition. Not until Larry Motz married Lynette Studebaker in 1963, did his mother present the quilt to the couple.[10]

Figure 5-15 *STREAK OF LIGHTNING, dated 192(?), unknown maker; cotton, pattern pieced, 58" x 79", Collection of Pam Eldridge, AQS 932a.*

Streak of Lightning

One of the endearing orphans of the survey is the Streak of Lightning quilt *(fig. 5.15)*. Amazingly, the quilt was purchased at a moving sale in Anchorage. Its history is unknown. The seller said, "I found this in my mother's trunk after she died. I kept the afghans I know she made. Somebody else made that one and I don't want it."[11] This orphan is an interesting example of how emotional family attachments to certain items can transcend or blind the viewer to another object's usefulness or beauty.

The Streak of Lightning is pieced with an assortment of scraps which form large triangles of various values. These, in turn, are staggered to compose the larger zigzags that alternate with the solid colored streaks. The quilt artist's random placement of the smaller negative and positive triangle groups impact the lightning streaks by making them either more or less prominent. The quilter's use of large solid pieces in contrast to the smaller pieced triangles creates an effectively bold design. Dark blue

Figure 5-16 *Charles and Julia Ann Jewell (seated) with their children standing left to right: Frank, John, and Ruth. Courtesy of Douglas and Bonnie Shaw.*

Figure 5-17 *Handpainted birth fraktur inscribed "Miss Julian Weller was born Febuary [sic] the 24th, 1840." Courtesy of Douglas and Bonnie Shaw.*

streaks zigzag powerfully down both sides of the quilt, and the central yellow streak creates the impression of heat and dimension. Although the quilt was made in the 1920s, the imposing graphics defy the stereotypical block designs from those years. Clearly, the quilter was not constrained by the typical piecing of blocks or the standard designs of the time.

The Seven Sisters Quilt

The Seven Sisters quilt *(fig. 5.18)*, in contrast, is precisely and meticulously pieced in fabrics typical of the late 1880s. All the corner points come together exactly as planned. The quiltmaker, Julia Ann (Weller) Copsey Jewell, was born in 1840; she married twice. Her first husband, Franklin Copsey, served in the Civil War and died of pneumonia. She lived in Bazine, Kansas, with her second husband, Charles Jewell. Julia Ann hand-pieced the Seven Sisters quilt in 1901 when she was 60.[12] Her signature, "Julia Jewell," appears in the center red star. Many of the quilts that she produced were made around the turn of the nineteenth century when she was ill and confined to bed. She is said to have spent her days making quilts as long as someone would thread the needle.

Although the Seven Sisters star clusters are each made from different fabrics, the artist placed them with care to highlight the red. The constellation of seven red groups of seven stars each takes center stage in the middle of the quilt. The various fabrics used for the darker star groups arouse interest as the supporting cast. When the colored stars recede into the background, the white hexagons float on a starry sky of red and blue. The strong red, white, and blue border contains the beautifully-pieced groups of seven sisters.

Figure 5-18 *Seven Sisters, dated and signed, "1901 Julia Jewell aged 61 years," Julia Ann (Weller) Copsey Jewell, Kansas; cotton, pattern pieced, 66" x 81", Collection of Douglas and Bonnie Shaw, AQS 1410a.*

Figure 5-19 *Ann (Hylton) Castle. Courtesy of Elizabeth Anne Castle Cole.*

Figure 5-20 *Summer and Winter pattern detail, 1900-1925, Ann Catherine Castle, Lakeside, Washington; cotton, pattern pieced, 81" x 85", Collection of Elizabeth Anne Castle Cole, AQS 97j.*

Inspired by Weaving Patterns

Quilt artists drew inspiration from a myriad of sources. Women in earlier times were responsible for producing textiles for their homes and families, so it was usual for women to weave, quilt, knit and produce various kinds of needlework. Ann (Hylton) Castle probably used one of her weaving patterns as the design basis for her yellow and black quilt. *(fig. 5-20)* The brilliant yellow and intense black are used to advantage, forming the unusual positive and negative interlocking circles. The coverlets that were handwoven in the eastern United States and Canada in the late 1800s were often of a "summer and winter" pattern, a reference to the contrasting light and dark values. One of the appealing aspects of Ann's quilt, however, is the unexpected color combination that defines the sharply contrasting pieces. The quilt is a stunning graphic piece that grabs the attention of the viewer. Although the pattern is typical of a traditionally woven piece, the colors give it a startlingly unorthodox look as a quilt.

This unconventional quiltmaker, Ann Catherine Hylton was born August 3, 1856 in Floyd, Virginia. She married Crocket Castle in 1880, when she was twenty-four. They traveled by train across country to settle in Glenwood Valley, Washington in 1894, completing the last portion of the journey on the *Bailey Gattchett*, a boat that plied the Columbia River. They homesteaded there, first in a log cabin, before moving to Lakeside, Washington where they built a large home and barns. It is thought that Ann Castle had nearly finished the yellow and black quilt when she died in 1926. It was subsequently finished by her daughter-in-law June S. Castle, and later presented to June's daughter, Elizabeth Anne Castle Cole, in 1970.[13]

(above) **Figure 5-21** *Miranda E. Ransburg (left) c.1915. Miranda loved to discuss politics and read the newspaper from top to bottom. The flu epidemic of 1917-1918 claimed her life. Courtesy of Larry and Karla Zervos.*

Figure 5-22 *Floral album, signed and dated, "Commenced Jan: 1879 Finished June 1879 By MER," Miranda E. Ransberg, b. 1846 (?), Maryland or Virginia; cotton, appliqué, 80" × 82", Collection of Larry and Karla Zervos, AQS 259s.*

A Beautiful Seamstress

Red and green appliqué quilts often were a quilter's *tour de force* among the more pragmatic bed coverings in a woman's collection. The rich color of the appliquéd pieces of Miranda E. Ransburg's quilt are now faded, and the ink signatures are barely readable, but the fine hand-quilted images still remain. Family history relates that "she was a beautiful seamstress — you could wear the dresses that she made inside out." The subject matter on the blocks is carefully recorded on a chart kept by descendants. Miranda seemed to take pleasure in the fruit of the earth and birds of the sky, as apple, peach, orange, and cherry trees are illustrated along with clover, oak leaves, and a Christmas cactus. One square has an appliquéd watermelon cut in half with the knife along side that did the cutting. Her pleasurable experiences with the natural world are revealed further by quilted hands picking fruit that birds also enjoy. With careful searching, stars and hearts can also be found.

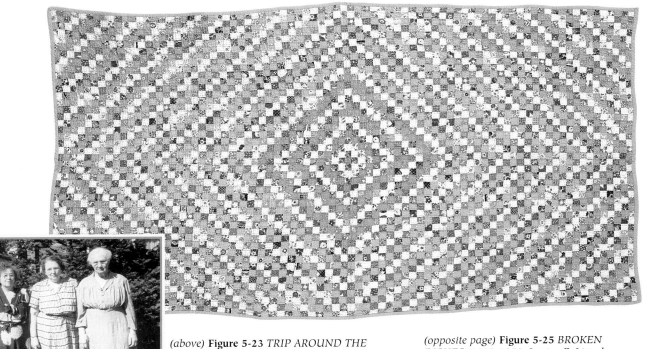

(above) **Figure 5-23** *TRIP AROUND THE WORLD, 1925-1950, Lavine P. Lincoln, Rock Island, Illinois; cotton, pattern pieced, 29" x 55", Collection of Carolyn Mustard, AQS 1286f.*

(opposite page) **Figure 5-25** *BROKEN DISHES, 1925-1950, Lavine P. Lincoln or Rozelle (Lincoln) Cox, Rock Island, Illinois; cotton, pattern pieced, 69" x 95", Collection of Carolyn Mustard, AQS 1289f.*

(above) **Figure 5-24** *From left: Lavine P. Lincoln, Rozelle (Lincoln) Cox, Mrs. Jeffers, Margaret A. Cox in the 1940s. Courtesy of Carolyn Mustard.*

Quilting Collaborators

Margaret (Arclarius) Cox, her daughter-in-law Rozelle (Lincoln) Cox and Rozelle's older unmarried sister, Lavine Lincoln, lived in the same house for thirty years, and much of that time they were making quilts together. They shared fabrics, and combined the same ones time and again in many different patterns. Margaret Cox, who was born in 1860, remembered being lifted to her father's shoulders to see President Abraham Lincoln as he was campaigning in Illinois for his second term. The longevity of this family seems to go hand in hand with an intense interest in quilt-making, as Lavine lived to be at least 100 years old, and Margaret lived to celebrate 105 years; Rozelle was only 82 when she died.[14]

The Trip Around the World quilt *(fig. 5.23)* Lavine created is an amazing example of an heirloom made with a child in mind. Objects made to a smaller scale for children have an indefinable charm. The quilt is only twenty-nine by fifty-five inches, but it contains hundreds of

pieces, set in concentric squares around a center cross. The darker gold pieces give way to sunny yellow rows. The printed and plain white squares between the yellow rows make the surface of the quilt twinkle. We can imagine that it provided many trips around the world of dreamland in the lives of the children who were lucky enough to have slept under it.

All three women had a unique sense of design and construction. Their creative use of fabric and adept choice of placement allowed them to use the simplest of shapes but create quilts that are visual treats. The quilt *(fig. 5.25)*, composed of identical right triangles, is a case in point. The triangles are actually fabric squares folded in half and then tightly whip-stitched to each other along the edges. In one stroke, this created a two-sided quilt. The vintage print triangles in medium and light shades are strung together in diagonal strips, and alternate with more intense and brightly colored strips of solid triangles. The ingenious

Figure 5-26 *CRAZY top, 1865-1890, signed "GLD,"*
Mary (Boni) Gaylord Donohue, Marine City,
Michigan; silk and velvet, irregular pieced, 53" x 64",
Collection of Caryl Lewis, AQS 1447a.

layout tends to cause the lighter print triangles to float on the surface of the quilt. Wide variations in the depth of color cause the solid triangles to "move" and recombine with their printed neighbors, depending on where they fall in the quilt. This quilt has an appealing combination of humble strength and powerful illusion that somehow springs from the simple triangle shape. The imaginative quilts of Lavine, Margaret, and Rozelle created a wonderful family legacy.

Bold and Crazy

Although a variety of Crazy quilts surfaced during the survey, one *(fig. 5.26)* made by Mary (Boni) Gaylord Donahue had a special charm. The artist constructed nine large Crazy-pieced blocks with unusual graphic qualities. The dark moon, for example, is a unique feature, as are the wonderfully imaginative pieced borders and the inset corners. The artist's strong sense of design is especially apparent in that she used a popular technique to create a bold graphic work. Elements typical of Crazy quilts appear, such as the extensive outline embroidery and lavishly worked initials. Rather than the cloying prettiness of most Victorian Crazy quilts, however, this quilt exhibits strength because of an almost architectural use of sumptuous, pieced fabrics framed by a dark, powerful border.

Mary Boni was born in Chautauqua County, New York in 1826 and eventually moved to Marine City, Michigan, where she died in 1890. A small Log Cabin quilt that she made in 1869 was taken west to Nebraska by family members in 1902. This vibrantly colored child's quilt was stolen by gypsies. One quarter of the quilt was later recovered by the sheriff and returned to the current owner's mother. She said, "They [the gypsies] liked nice things for their babies."[15]

More Than the Sum of Its Parts

The exact nature of any quilt's appeal is difficult to define. Some quilts are bold; some are gorgeous. Many have a seductive quality that lures admirers to return again and again. What an instructive and entertaining revelation it would be if we could magically extract each quiltmaker's thoughts during the design process, and if we were able to share in the agony and delight of making color and fabric choices.

Chuck Close, an innovative modern artist who favors the nineteenth century painter Georges Seurat's dots of color, but on a grander scale, talks about combining small increments to produce an entire image. "I believe Seurat set up his process as a method of operation and then was immediately swept away into an intuitive level. This method of making something incrementally is similar to the way I have been working. I have a lot of self-imposed limitations and rules, but within my superimposed order, there's tremendous freedom."[16] Close's thoughts seem to reflect the process used by many quiltmakers, both past and present, to create a fantastic composite that evokes an emotional response. Something more than the sum of the parts results from sewing together the least significant fabric bits. The potential to freely create that resides in this mysterious process ensures the continuation of creative quiltmaking.

(above) Unnamed pattern, 1865-1900, unknown maker, possibly made in New York; cotton, pattern pieced, 85" x 86", Collection of Rachel Adkins, AQS 1130f. This quilt was found in the owner's great grandparents' Etna, New York home.

(opposite page) YANKEE PUZZLE, 1865-1900, unknown maker; cotton, pattern pieced, 67" x 82", Collection of Ginny Packer, AQS 395s.

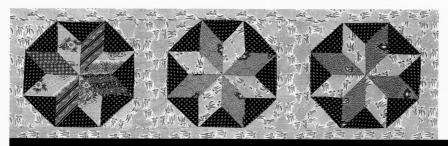

OCTAGON STAR detail, 1865-1900, attributed to Mabel (Harris) Hisken, possibly New York; cotton, pattern pieced, 78" x 80", Collection of Shirley Coursey, AQS 994a. The purple in the wisteria of the background print has largely faded to brown.

AQS DATABASE

THE ALASKA QUILT SURVEY used the Macintosh FileMaker Pro program for its computer database. The record numbers in the database run through 1-1557. However, the total number of actual quilts registered was 1,528. The unused record numbers that had been held in reserve for future use were eliminated. Other quilt records that had insufficient information for analysis were also eliminated. Therefore, the total number of quilt records used in the database searches was 1,523. The seventy-three fields of each quilt record were divided into two parts — a history section and a quilt data section. The forms used during Discovery Days were also divided in these two parts. Most fields had a choice of entries in the form of pre-defined "pop-up" menus or a set selection of choices.

HISTORY SECTION

Field name:
- registry number
- last name
- first name
- address
- city
- state
- zip
- telephone
- participant type, ie. owner
- when moved to Alaska
- why moved to Alaska
- city quilt made
- state quilt made
- country quilt made
- how quilt acquired
- how related to quiltmaker
- quilt related items owned
- quiltmaker married last name
- quiltmaker first name
- quiltmaker maiden name
- location quiltmaker born
- birth date quiltmaker
- death date quiltmaker
- ethnic heritage quiltmaker
- family/familiar pattern name
- source of design
- how maker learned to quilt
- other quiltmakers in family
- number of people making quilt
- purpose of quilt, i.e. utilitarian
- why quilt was made, i.e. keep hands busy
- exhibit permission
- educational permission

QUILT DATA SECTION

Field name:
- quilt status, ie. complete bed quilt
- size in inches
- condition, ie. like new
- exceptional example, ie. design
- attributed quilt date
- estimated era of quilt, ie. 1900-1925
- quilt date inscribed
- design method of top, ie. pieced with applique
- Brackman pieced encyclopedia volume number
- Brackman pieced encyclopedia pattern number
- irregular pieced top
- type of appliqué
- Brackman appliqué number
- pattern name 1
- pattern name 2
- general quilt description
- color choice, ie. traditional for era
- quilt materials, ie. wool
- materials manufactured, ie. homespun
- top construction method, ie. hand
- quilt signed
- method of signing
- sash
- border
- surface decoration, ie. embroidery
- method of quilting, ie. hand
- stitches per inch
- style of quilting, ie. elaborate
- filling
- oral recording
- color reproduction
- black and white reproduction

Embroidered bird and initials on the back of the CRAZY quilt, Venetia (Fehr) Pugh Reed, AQS 960a. (Also see p. 31.)

AQS DATABASE

Northern Bound

Out of the 1500 survey participants who responded to the question about when they moved to Alaska, only 86 had moved to the state before 1950. Between 1951-1970, 350 individual survey participants moved to the state. The trans-Alaska oil pipeline created an economic boom in the 1970s, and 1,064 people answered that they moved to Alaska during that period. The majority of people of any era responded that they moved to Alaska for economic opportunity.

The survey emphasized quilts made before 1959, and as we suspected most early quilts were brought into the state. The quilts were made in almost all of the "lower 48" states (none from Hawaii). The state of origin for most quilts was unknown by the participants but the largest numbers were attributed to Oregon (64), Washington (59), Illinois (57), Pennsylvania (50) and California (46). States credited with between 30-40 quilts each were Missouri and Oklahoma. Ohio, Nebraska, New York, Kentucky, Iowa and Idaho contributed at least twenty quilts each. Many quilts arrived as family heirlooms, and 760 quilts were inherited while 157 quilts were gifts from a relative. Unfortunately, answers to ethnic back ground was not accurate enough to be useful.

The majority of the 1,523 quilts analyzed were not made in Alaska. Only 337 registered quilts were made in Alaska, and out of that number only three came to light as being made before 1900. Five Alaskan-made quilts were registered between 1900 and 1925; only 19 quilts were documented as Alaskan-made from 1925-1950; 180 quilts turned up as made in Alaska between 1950 and 1970.

Dating Results

The tally of nineteenth century quilts in the survey was 195 or about thirteen percent of the total. Only 21 quilts before 1900 were actually inscribed with a date. Four quilts were assigned to the 1800-1840 era. For the period including the Civil War, 1840-1865, 27 registered quilts could be assigned. An increase in quiltmaking was reflected by the 164 quilts placed in the era from 1865 to 1900. We assigned 159 quilts to 1900-1925, though this era seemed to be the most difficult to determine. As part of the popular quilt revival era of 1925 to 1950, 606 quilts were registered. Quilts with Alaskan themes or designs did not appear until the early 1970s.

Design and Construction

The widespread popularity of some quilt patterns became obvious after only a few Discovery Days. Crazy quilts were highest in number with 81 of this style documented. The Grandmother's Flower Garden, in its many variations, was the next most registered pattern, and 70 were counted. Then following in order of pattern occurrence were the Double Wedding Ring, Nine Patch, Log Cabin, Dresden Plate and Irish Chain. Pieced patterns were by far the most popular method of construction, and they numbered 1,283. Of these, 213 quilts were combined with appliqué. Whole top appliqué quilts numbered 54. Hand quilting was exceptional on many quilts in the survey, and 81 quilts had 10 to 16 stitches to the inch (counted as a single stitch on the top of the quilt in at least two places). Only six of these 81 quilts had 14 to 16 stitches to the inch.

The database will eventually be made available in research libraries of Alaska. We hope to incorporate the quilt images with the database in a CD-ROM format.

ROBBING PETER TO PAY PAUL, 1865-1900, Mrs. Morrison, Missouri; cotton, pattern pieced and appliqué, 77" x 82", Collection of Tom Pearson, AQS 1383ko.

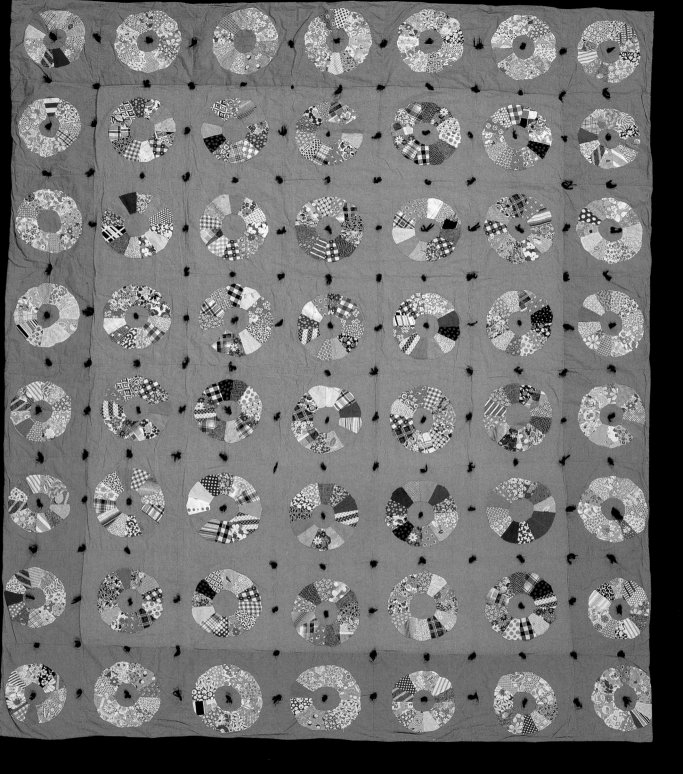

THE DESSERT PLATE, 1938-1955, Aleen Brown, Kansas; cotton, pattern pieced, 71" x 82", Collection of Aleen Brown. AQS 1262c. This quilt was started at age fourteen with scraps of clothing and was intended as a marriage quilt.

ENDNOTES

CHAPTER 1

1 Information learned from research, especially from C. L. Andrews, *The Story of Sitka* (Seattle, Washington: Loman & Hamford Co., 1992); Hector Chevigny, *Russian America: The Great Alaskan Venture, 1741-1867* (Portland, Oregon: Binford & Mort, Thomas Binford, Publisher, 1965); R. N. DeArmond, ed., *Lady Franklin Visits Sitka, Alaska 1870: The Journal of Sophia Cracroft Sir John Franklin's Niece* (Anchorage, Alaska: Alaska Historical Society, 1981).

2 "The traditions of patchwork art was laid in Russia in the nineteenth century. This was connected with the popularization of mass produced chintz.... [Everyday] blankets were not sewn from new fabrics, but from pieces of old clothing and domestic objects which had long outlived their original purpose. And to this day a necessary condition for the creation of a quilt is that one-third of the materials comes from scraps." Yevgenia Petrova, Editor-in-Chief, *Russian Patchwork* (St. Petersburg: State Russian Museum, 1997).

3 Wendy Jones, *Women Who Braved The North* (San Diego, California: Grossmount Press, Inc., 1976), 27.

4 Eliza Ruhamah Scidmore, *Appletons' Guide-Book To Alaska and The Northwest Coast* (New York: D. Appleton and Company, 1893), 116.

5 Jones, 27.

6 Kyrill Khlebnikov, *Colonial Russian America, Reports 1817-32* (Glass-Dahlstrom Printers: Oregon Historical Society, 1976), 13-64.

7 DeArmond, xxiii.

8 Lyman Woodman, *Duty Station Northwest: U.S. Army In Alaska and Western Canada, 1867-1917*, Vol. I (Anchorage, Alaska: Alaska Historical Society, 1996), 35.

9 *Alta California*, 12 November 1867 cited in Woodman, 36.

10 Ibid.

11 Andrews, Chevigny, DeArmond.

12 DeArmond, 93-124.

13 C. Kurt Dewhurst, Betty MacDowell, and Marsha MacDowell, *Artists in Aprons* (New York: E.P. Dutton, 1979).

14 Betty John, *Libby: The Sketches, Letters & Journal of Libby Beaman, Recorded in the Pribilof Islands 1879-1880 as Presented by Her Granddaughter Betty John* (Tulsa, Oklahoma: Council Oak Books, 1987), 18.

15 Ibid., 71.

16 Ibid., 72.

17 Ibid., 195.

18 Eva McClintock, *Life In Alaska: Letters of Mrs. Eugene S. Willard* (Philadelphia: Presbyterian Board of Publications, 1884), 363.

19 Alaska State Museum, Catalog Record, 24 July 1985.

20 *History of Nodaway County, Missouri* (St. Joseph, Missouri: National Historical Society, 1882), 385.

21 *The Alaskan*, 26 May 1888.

22 *North Star*, September 1888, 38.

23 *North Star*, July 1888, 31.

24 "Local Jottings," *Juneau City Mining Record*, 11 December 1890, 5.

25 *North Star*, July 1888, 31.

26 *North Star*, March 1895, 2.

27 *The Alaskan*, 1885-1897.

28 DeArmond, 108.

29 Woodman, 32.

30 A painting in the collection of the Royal College of Surgeons, London, "Private Thomas Walker sewing a cloth Coverlet in Fort Pitt Military Hospital in 1856" illustrates this tradition. It is reproduced as Figure 152 in Averil Colby's book *Patchwork*.

31 Janet Rae and Margaret Tucker, "Quilts with Special Associations," in Janet Rae et al, *Quilt Treasures of Great Britain*. (Nashville, Tennessee: Rutledge Hill Press, 1995), 170-172.

32 Veterans Records, Company K, 104th Regiment N.Y. Infantry, National Archives, Washington, D.C.

33 Mrs. Richard (Marilyn) Curtis, written information from Accession Records 1984.0406.01, Division of Textiles, Smithsonian Institution National Museum of American History, Cindy Pentony, Museum Technician, to Mary Ann Vaughan, 22 February 2000.

34 "The Famed 14th, Vancouver's Favorite, 1893-1917," article by Ted Van Arsdol in *Clark County History*, Fort Vancouver Historical Society, 1972, 202.

35 Woodman, 144.

36 *Dyea Trail*, 25 February 1898.

37 Mary Bywater Cross, telephone conversation with June E. Hall, 12 November 2000.

38 Ibid.

39 Curtis.

40 Cross.

41 Martha Louise Black, *My Ninety Years*, ed. Flo Whyard (Anchorage, Alaska: Alaska Northwest Publishing Company, 1976), 18.

42 Clare Rudolf Murphy and Jane G. Haigh, *Gold Rush Women* (Anchorage, Alaska: Alaska Northwest Books, 1997), 15.

43 Sandra Myres, "Women of The American West," *Women In Alaska History*, No.70, Seminar of the Alaska Historical Commission Studies in History (Anchorage, Alaska: Alaska Historical Society, 1983), 8.

44 *Report On Population and Resources of Alaska at the Eleventh Census: 1890* (Washington, D.C.: Government Printing Office, 1893), 3.

45 Myres, 8.

46 Marie Quirk Haggard, conversation with author Ruth Jolly Knapmau, *Klondike—Pioneer Rediscovery, Pioneers of Alaska*, 82nd Grand Igloo Convention, September 9-12 (1998), Dawson, Yukon Territory.

47 Courtney Linkous, letter to Willette Janes, March 2000.

48 *The Alaskan*, 1888.

49 Frances Backhouse, *Women of The Klondike* (Vancouver, Canada: Whitecap Books, 1995), 65.

50 Ibid.

51 Lorene Gordon, correspondence with Willette Janes, 16 March 2000.

52 Jones, 88.

53 Gordon.

[54] Jane Scott Perkins, telephone conversation with Willette Janes, 9 and 20 April 2000.

[55] Karl Hahn, correspondence with Willette Janes, 2 April 2000.

[56] Ken and Morrison Coates, *The Sinking of The Princess Sophia: Taking The North Down With Her* (Fairbanks, Alaska: University of Alaska Press, 1991), 58.

[57] W. M. Dynes, *Dynes' Alaska Directory and Buyers Guide: Juneau*, 1921, Section 21, 63.

[58] *Alaska Daily Empire* (Juneau), 25 February 1924.

[59] Hahn.

CHAPTER

[1] Betty John, *Libby: The Sketches, Letters & Journal of Libby Beaman, Recorded in the Pribilof Islands 1879-1880 as Presented by her Granddaughter Betty John* (Tulsa, Oklahoma: Council Oak Books, 1987), 72.

[2] Pauline Wilson written correspondence to June E. Hall, 23 May 2000.

[3] Clipping from unknown Baton Rouge newspaper, courtesy of Barrow Morgan family.

[4] Bob Burke, *From Oklahoma to Eternity The Life of Wiley Post* (Oklahoma City: Oklahoma Heritage Association, 1998), 199.

[5] AQS written documentation #1290ke, 22 February 1998.

[6] Selma Giesler, telephone conversation with June E. Hall, 14 August 1997.

[7] Flora R. Corbin, letter to Wilma Corbin Mason, 18 April 1932, Cornell, Illinois.

[8] Mary Albright, telephone conversation with June E. Hall, 13 January 1998.

[9] AQS written documentation #829a, 3 October 1998.

[10] Thelma Spence, personal manuscript, c.1975.

[11] Ibid.

[12] AQS written documentation #1108f, 11 November 1997.

[13] AQS written documentation #74j, 11 July 1992.

[14] AQS written documentation #900a, 28 September 1998.

[15] AQS written documentation #406s, 29 January 1994.

[16] AQS written documentation #139j, 11 July 1992.

[17] *The Detroit News*, 16 October 1934.

[18] Ibid.

[19] Ibid.

[20] Marjorie Colpitts, AQS taped interview, 26 January 1997.

CHAPTER

[1] US Bureau of the Census, *U. S. Census of Population: 1950. Vol. II Characteristics of the Population. Parts 51-4 Territories and Possessions* (Washington, DC: US Government Printing Office, 1953), 51-4; and *Fifteenth Census of the United States: 1930, Outlying Territories and Possessions: Number and Distribution of Inhabitants* (Washington, DC: US Government Printing Office, 1932), 8, 15.

[2] Claus-M. Naske and Herman E. Slotnick, *Alaska: A History of the 49th State*, 2nd ed. (Norman: University of Oklahoma Press, 1987), 97.

[3] Steve W. Brown, *Fact Book: 1996* (Fairbanks: University of Alaska Fairbanks, 1996), 1-3.

[4] US Bureau of the Census, *Fifteenth Census*, 15.

[5] Evangeline Atwood, "Pioneer Banker," *Alaska Journal Vol. 8, No. 1* (Winter 1978): 27-28.

[6] Elmer Rasmuson, letter to Dorothy DeWar, Skagway Museum, 1966.

[7] S. Jane Szabo, "Spectacular Piece of History: Rasmuson duck 'robe' is prized find for Alaska Quilt Survey," *Anchorage Daily News*, 4 October 1997, D-2.

[8] Lydia Fohn-Hansen, her column in *Jesson's Weekly*, (195?), Lydia Fohn-Hansen Collection, Elmer E. Rasmuson Library Archives, Fairbanks.

[9] Szabo, D-2.

[10] William Olssen, telephone conversation with June Hall, 31 March 2000.

[11] Peggy Petersen Arness, interview by Kathy Wartinbee, Kenai, Alaska, February 2000.

[12] Mae Annette Fox Sharp (granddaughter of Florence), author of unpublished family history, Olympia, Washington.

[13] Arness.

[14] Sharp.

[15] Louise McDonald, "Patching Together a Personal History," *Peninsula Clarion*, 22 February 1998, A-10.

[16] Sharp and McDonald.

[17] McDonald.

[18] *Fairbanks Daily News-Miner*, 18 September 1924, 4.

[19] Premium books stored at the Tanana Valley Fair Association office, Fairbanks.

[20] Premium books, Elmer E. Rasmuson Library, Fairbanks.

[21] US Bureau of the Census, *U. S. Census of Population: 1950*, 51-4.

[22] *The Cooperative Extension Service: Past, Present and Future, 1978-79*, [iv].

[23] Photographs in the Fohn-Hansen Collection, Rasmuson Library Archives, Fairbanks, show samples of her excellent work.

[24] April 18, 1933, Fohn-Hansen Collection, Box 4, Folder 13, ACC#90-130.

[25] The quilt block was "made by Mrs. Reese Collins' sister." Fohn-Hansen Collection, Photographs 90-130-007 and 90-130-008.

[26] "News Letter to Homemakers," Vol. II, December 1932, Fohn-Hansen Collection, Box 8.

[27] "News Letter to Homemakers," April 1933, Fohn-Hansen Collection, Box 8.

[28] Florence O'Neill Imlach and Leslie Wien Hajdukovich, conversation with Dana F. Bowne, 26 April 2000; price of fabric from Frances and Harry Walton Papers, Letters 1923-52, Series 1, Box 1, University of Alaska Anchorage Library Archives.

[29] "News Letter to Homemakers," April 1933, Fohn-Hansen Collection, Box 8.

[30] *The (Juneau) Daily Empire*, advertisement, 20 Sept. 1916, 5.

[31] "News Letter to Homemakers," April 1942, 3, Fohn-Hansen Collection, Box 8.

[32] "News Letter to Homemakers," April 1933, Fohn-Hansen Collection, Box 8.

[33] Lydia Fohn-Hansen to Ruth O'Brien, the Chief of the Division of Textiles and Clothing for Home Economics, U.S. Dept of Home Economics, 31 May 1935, Fohn-Hansen Collection, Box 4.

[34] "Women Storm Quilt Show to Examine Masterpieces," *The Detroit News*, 13 Oct 1934.

[35] Naske and Slotnick, 112-114.

[36] Newspaper clipping, 11 November 1935, unknown source, in Cooperative Extension Service Collection, Box 24, Clippings 1931-1940.

[37] Frances Walton to her mother, 1936, Frances and Harry Walton Papers, Letters 1923-52, Series 1, Box 1, University of Alaska Anchorage Library Archives.

[38] *The Valley Settler*, 1 July 1938, 9.

[39] US Bureau of the Census, *U. S. Census of Population: 1950*, 51-4.

[40] Connie Davis, written information, 10 Nov. 1999.

[41] Fohn-Hansen Collection, Box 8.

[42] Mrs. J. C. Thomas, "Every Woman Should Have a Part in Red Cross Work," transcript of a radio talk rpt. in *The Alaska Woman 2*, (November 1942): 12.

[43] US Bureau of the Census, *U. S. Census of Population: 1950*, 51-4.

[44] "Textile Exhibits Invited for Fair," *Fairbanks Daily News-Miner*, 23 August 1948, 3.

[45] Premium books, Elmer E. Rasmuson Library, Fairbanks.

[46] US Bureau of the Census, *U. S. Census of Population: 1960, Vol. I, Characteristics of the Population. Part 3 Alaska* (Washington, DC: US Government Printing Office, 1963), 3-17.

[47] "Homemakers Clubs Planning Programs," *Fairbanks Daily News-Miner*, 16 April 1956, 6.

[48] Peggy Goodfellow, "Alaska Homemakers Clubs Report Latest News Items," *Fairbanks Daily News-Miner*, 21 April 1954, 6.

[49] "General Report of Fifth Annual Short Course for Homemakers, University of Alaska, October 1954" (mimeographed), Fohn-Hansen Collection, Box 4, Folder 27.

[50] "Sixth Annual Homemakers' Short Course Notes," 1955 (mimeographed), Fohn-Hansen Collection, Box 4, Folder 27.

[51] "Extension Homemaker Club Activities for the Past Year as Reported by the Presidents. 1958 (mimeographed), Fohn-Hansen Collection, Box 4, Folder 23.

[52] Newsletters issued daily during Homemakers' Short Courses at UAF 1953 (mimeographed), Fohn-Hansen Collection, Box 4, Folder 27.

[53] Alice Sherwood Johnstone, telephone conversation with June E. Hall, 23 June 1999.

[54] Fohn-Hanson Collection, Box 4, Folder 26 (mimeographed).

[55] For example, see Betsy Woodman, *50 Golden Years: The Story of the Anchorage Women's Club*, 1965.

CHAPTER 4

[1] John Middleton, *Clothing in Colonial Russian America: A New Look* (Kingston, Ontario: Limestone Press, 1996), 30.

[2] George T. Emmons, *The Tlingit Indian* (Seattle: University of Washington Press, 1991), 323; Eva McClintock, *Life in Alaska: Letters of Mrs. Eugene S. Willard* (Philadelphia: Presbyterian Board of Publications, 1884), 32-36.

[3] Middleton, 121.

[4] R.N. DeArmond, ed. *Lady Franklin Visits Sitka, Alaska 1870: The Journal of Sophia Cracroft Sir Franklin's Niece* (Anchorage, Alaska: Alaska Historical Society, 1981), 25.

[5] McClintock, 326.

[6] *North Star*, March 1895, 2.

[7] Emma Widmark, conversation with June E. Hall, 6 September 2000.

[8] Cecilia Kunz, conversations with June E. Hall, 23 August 2000, 12 September 2000.

[9] Ann Fienup-Riordan, *The Nelson Island Eskimo: Social Structure and Ritual Distribution* (Anchorage, Alaska: Alaska Pacific University Press, 1983).

CHAPTER 5

[1] Hilda Stoltzfus, letter to June E. Hall February, 2000.

[2] AQS written documentation #175j, 12 March 1999.

[3] AQS written documentation #81j, 11 July 1992.

[4] Fruit Basket newspaper article from Ruby McKim Studies, 1932, via Merikay Waldvogel.

[5] AQS written documentation #679w, 8 February 1997.

[6] AQS written documentation #1277f, 18 April 1998.

[7] AQS written documentation #1497f, 16 May 1998.

[8] AQS written documentation #771v, 31 May 1997.

[9] AQS written documentation #899a, 4 October 1997.

[10] Lynette Motz, letter to June E. Hall, 15 June 1998.

[11] AQS written documentation #932a, 14 October 1997.

[12] Bonnie Shaw, letter to June E. Hall, 20 May 1998.

[13] Elizabeth A. Cole, written information to Mary Ann Vaughan, March 2000.

[14] Carolyn Mustard, telephone interview with June E. Hall, 31 August 2000.

[15] AQS written documentation #1447a, 16 May 1998.

[16] Patrick Pacheco, "Point Counterpoint," *Art and Antiques* (October 1991).

Ink drawings of AQS quilt patterns by Carol Thilenius, 1992.

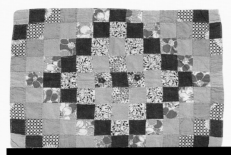

AROUND THE WORLD doll quilt, 1927, Cora
(Belt) Roberts or Amelia Roberts, Spokane,
Washington; cotton, pattern pieced, 10" x 15",
Collection of Patty Bickar, AQS 197s.

SELECTED BIBLIOGRAPHY

Alaska Quilt Survey: 1992-2000. Documents 1-1557.

Black, Martha Louise. *My Ninety Years*. Edited by Flo Whyard. Anchorage, Alaska: Alaska Northwest Publishing Company, 1976.

Bowman, Doris. *The Smithsonian Treasury: American Quilts*. Washington, D.C.: Smithsonian Press, 1991.

Brackman, Barbara. *Clues in the Calico: A Guide to the Identifying and Dating Antique Quilts*. McLean, Virginia: EMP Publications, 1989.

Brackman, Barbara. *Encyclopedia of Appliqué*. McLean, Virginia: EPM Publications, Inc., 1993.

Brackman, Barbara. *An Encyclopedia of Pieced Quilt Patterns*. 8 vols. Lawrence, Kansas: Prairie Flower Publishing, 1979-1984.

Burke, Bob. *From Oklahoma to Eternity: The Life of Wiley Post*. Oklahoma City: Oklahoma Heritage Association, 1998.

Chevigny, Hector. *Russian America: The Great Alaskan Venture, 1741-1867*. Portland, Oregon: Binford & Mort, Thomas Binford Publisher, 1965.

Coates, Ken and Morrison Coates. *The Sinking of the Princess Sophia: Taking the North Down with Her*. Fairbanks, Alaska: University of Alaska Press, 1991.

DeArmond, R.N., ed. *Lady Franklin Visits Sitka, Alaska 1870: The Journal of Sophia Cracroft, Sir John Franklin's Niece*. Anchorage, Alaska: Alaska Historical Society, 1981.

Dewhurst, C. Kurt, Betty MacDowell, and Marsha MacDowell. *Artists in Aprons*. New York: E.P. Dutton, 1979.

Emmons, George T. *The Tlingit Indian*. Seattle: University of Washington Press, 1991.

Hall, Carrie A., and Rose G. Kretsinger. *The Romance of the Patchwork Quilt in America*. New York: Bonanza Books, 1935.

Holstein, Jonathan. *Abstract Design in American Quilts: A Biography of an Exhibition*. Louisville, Kentucky: The Kentucky Quilt Project, 1991.

Horton, Laurel, ed. *Quiltmaking in America: Beyond the Myths, Selected Writings from the American Quilt Study Group*. Nashville, Tennessee: Rutledge Hill Press, 1994.

John, Betty, ed. *Libby: The Sketches, Letters, & Journal of Libby Beaman, Recorded in the Pribilof Islands, 1879-1880 as Presented by Her Granddaughter Betty John*. Tulsa, Oklahoma: Council Oak Books, 1987.

Kiracoff, Roderick. *The American Quilt: A History of Cloth and Comfort, 1750-1950*. New York: Clarkson Potter, 1993.

Khlebnikov, Kyrill. *Colonial Russian America, Reports 1817-32*. Glass-Dahlstrom Printers, Oregon Historical Society, 1976.

Lydia Fohn-Hansen Collection. Elmer E. Rasmuson Library, University of Alaska Fairbanks.

MacDowell, Marsha and C. Kurt Dewhurst. *To Honor and Comfort: Native Quilting Traditions*. Santa Fe: Museum of New Mexico Press, 1997.

McClintock, Eva. *Life in Alaska: Letters of Mrs. Eugene S. Willard*. Philadelphia: Presbyterian Board of Publications, 1884.

Middleton, John. *Clothing in Colonial Russian America: A New Look*. Kingston, Ontario: Limestone Press, 1996.

Naske, Claus-M. and Herman E. Slotnick. *Alaska: A History of the 49th State*, 2nd ed. Norman: University of Oklahoma Press, 1987.

Petrova, Yevgenia, Editor-in-Chief. *Russian Patchwork*. St. Petersburg, Russia: State Russian Museum, 1997.

Rae, Janet et al. *Quilt Treasures of Great Britain: The Heritage Search of the Quilters' Guild*. Nashville, Tennessee: Rutledge Hill Press. 1995.

Safford, Carleton L. and Robert Bishop. *America's Quilts and Coverlets*. New York: Weathervane Books, 1974.

Scidmore, Eliza Ruhamah. *Appletons' Guide-Book to Alaska and the Northwest Coast*. New York: D. Appleton and Company, 1893.

Waldvogel, Merikay. *Softcovers for Hard TImes: Quiltmaking and the Great Depression*. Nashville, Tennessee: Rutledge Hill Press, 1990.

Woodman, Lyman. *Duty Station Northwest: U.S. Army in Alaska and Western Canada, 1867-1917*. Vol. I. Anchorage, Alaska: Alaska Historical Society, 1996.

Red Work child's quilt details, 1910-1945, George Stickroth, Olive Winans and Audrey Stickroth, Ohio; cotton, 67" x 94", Collection of Barbara Massenburg, AQS 694k.

The characters on this quilt were embroidered by Olive and George when they were children, and George was ill. George's wife, Audrey, put the squares together many years later.

CRAZY detail, dated and signed, "1885 MRD,"
Mary Rebecca (Kautz) Diller (1831-1898),
Lancaster, Pennsylvania; silk, satin, velvet
and ribbons, irregular pieced, 85" x 85",
Collection of Ned Strange, AQS 843a.

INDEX

*(Page numbers in **bold face** refer to illustrations and captions.)*

A

Abby Aldrich Rockefeller
   Folk Art Museum, 7, 26
Alaska Humanities Forum, 7, 13
The Alaskan, 27
Alaska Quilt Survey, 10, 12
Alaska Railroad, 57
Alaska State Museum, 7, 13
Alaska Treadwell Gold Mining Company, **19**
Album/Roman Cross, 53
Anchorage Museum of History and Art, 6
Around the World, **110**
At'oow, 73
Austin, Isabella (Mrs. Alonzo E.), 22

B

Baker, Mrs. R.M., **23**, 23
Barge, Lydia, **84**, 85
Beaman, Elizabeth "Libby" (Debois), 19,
   31, 35
Bering, Vitus, 17
Black, Louise Martha, 26
Bottemueller, Mrs., **88**, 89
Brackman, Barbara, 12
Brady, Elizabeth J., **20**, 22
Broken Dishes, 98, **99**
Brown, Aleen, **106**
Button blanket, **72**, 72

C

Cabin Fever Quilters Guild, 6
Cactus Basket, **4**
Capital City Quilters, 6
Carrie McLain Memorial Museum, 6
Castle, Ann (Hylton), **96**, 96
Catron, Lucy (Rash), **90**, 90
Cracroft, Sophia, 72
Chicago Century of Progress Exhibition,
   41, **50**
Chief Shakes, **70**
Chief Snake Quilt, **92**, 93
Child's Quilts, **26**, 27, **28**, 29, **66**, 66, **67**,
   110, **112**
Chilkoot Pass, 27
Chynoweth, Dolly, **5**
Civil War, 25
Clark, Catherine Monroe (March), **34**, 35
Colpitts, Marjorie (Grant), 52, 55, **55**
Corbin, Flora Cecelia (Rhodes), **40**, 41
Cordova Historical Museum and Library, 6
Cox, Roselle (Lincoln), **98**, 98

Crazy,   3, **5**, **12**, **20**, 21, **22**, **26**, 30, **30**,
   31, **31**, 38, **38**, **45**, 66, **67**, **83**, 85, **89**,
   89, 101, **100**, **111**, **112**
Crazy (Child's Quilt), 66, **67**
Cross, Mary Bywater, 25
Curtis, Jewett Washington, 25, 26

D

Darlin, Lillie, **63**, 63
Davis, Carol (Beery), **65**, 65
Davis, General Jefferson C., 25
Dawson Crazy, **20-23**
Dawson, Judge Lafayette, 21-23
DeArmond, Elizabeth (Davidson), **62**, 62
DeArmond, Robert N., 18, 23
DeGraf, Anna, 27
De Gruyter, Jeanette (Waring), **29**, 29
Denali, (Mt. McKinley), **14**
Dessert Plate, **106**
Detroit News Quilt Club Contest, **50**, 50
Diamond in the Square, **2**
Diamond Star, 61
Dickerson, Mildred, **54**
Diller, Mary Rebecca (Kautz), **111**
Discovery Days, 10, 11, 13, 81
Doll quilts, **48**, 48, **110**
Donahue, Mary (Boni) Gaylord, 101
Dorcas Society, **21**
Double Wedding Ring, **42**, 43
Downs, Marie, **48**, 48
Dresden Plate, **69**
Duck Neck Quilt, **56-58**, 58

E

Eagle clan, **70**
Eight-Pointed Star, **32**
Eisenhauer, Brian Ronald Dwight, **47**, 47
Emmons, George, **73**
Endless Chain, **88**, 89
Etholen, Lady Margaretha and Arvid, 18
Extension Service, **60**, 63, 68

F

Fairs, Alaskan, **60**, 60, 63, 67
Fan, **80-82**, 82, 85, 86
Floral Album, **97**, 97
Floral appliqué, **59**, 59
Flour sack, Eskimo Brand, **61**
Fohn-Hansen, Lydia Jacobson, 60, 61
French Bouquet, **55**, 55
Friends of the Alaska State Museum, 7, 13

Friends of the Wrangell Museum, 6
Friendship Skirt, 68
Fruit Basket, 86, **87**

G

Garden Path, **40**, 41
Gastineau Channel Historical Society, 6, 12
Gee, Beatrice and Arnold, **70**
Gold Rush, 25-27, 57
Goodell, Hannah (Griswold), 46
Grandmother's Flower Garden, **36**, 36,
   61, 86, **86**
Grant, Alice (Mrs. Whitaker M.), 22
Grant, Mary Catherine (Geddes), **32**
Grant, Ruth (Ingalls), **54**, 54

H

Hahn, Jennie (Austin), 63-65, **64**
Hammelbacher, Florence Olssen, **59**, 59
Hanford, Mary Stewart "Matie" (Gage), 12
Haydon, M.F. (Mary), 22
Hexagon, **10**, **66**, 66
Hisken, Mabel (Harris), **104**
Hodgins, Josephine, 66, **67**, 67
Holstein, Jonathan, 9
Homemakers Clubs, 67, 68
House Jack Built, **7**

I

Ikenberry, Margaret, **70**
Ingalls, Georgia S., **52**, 52

J

Jack in the Beanstalk, **112**
Jackson, Sheldon, 21
Jewell, Julia Ann (Weller) Copsey, **94**, 94
Jones, Martha (McCoy), 43
Joseph's Coat, **63**, 63
Juneau-Douglas City Museum, **13**, **62**

K

Katzeek, Anna, 73
Kenai Peninsula Piecemakers Quilt Group, 6
Kenton family quilters, 93
Kenton, Una (Mount), **92**, 93
Khlebnikov, Kryill, 72
Kidd, Leanna, 50, 51
Klein, Ron, **14**
Kodiak Bear Paw Quilters, 6
Kostrometinoff, Natalia and George, **23**, 23
Kuhns, Emma V., **49**, 49
Kunkel, Elizabeth (Robinson), **49**, 49
Kunkel, Evelyn and Eliza A., **49**, 49
Kunz, Cecilia, **70**, 73

L

Ladies of Alaska, **4**, **20**
Lang, Lydia, Lavina, Angie, **90**, 90
Lee, Rhoda, **20**, 22
Lincoln, Lavine P., **98**, 98
Log Cabin, **16**, **17**, **27**, 27, **44**, 44, **90**, 90
Log Cabin Child's Quilt, **28**, 29
Log Cabin Quilters, **6**

M

Martens, Geneva Lee (Steele), 50, 51
Matanuska Valley Colony, 62-63
McGranahan, Bessie Florence (Beyer), 85
McIllree, Harriet E. (Dearing), 69
McKim, Ruby, 62, 86, **87**
Mills, Ura Birdie (Conkle), **39**, 39
Missouri Beauty, **49**, 49
Modernistic Flower Quilt, 52, **54**
Morgan, Stanley, **36**, 36
Morrison, Mrs., **105**
Mosiac, **34**, 35
Motz, Naomi (Kenton), **92**, 93
Mullen, C., 54
Myres, Sandra (Dr.), 27

N

Nelly Don fabrics, 86
Nelson Island, **74**, 74
New York Beauty, 93
North Star, 21, 22
Northwest Passage, 31

O

Ocean Wave Quilters, 6, 13
Octagon Star, **104**
O'Neill, Florence (Leahy), 61
One Patch, **76**
Oregonian, 52
Overend, Josie (Mrs. Charles), **20**, 22

P

Pakle, Jennie, **20**, 22
Pennant, **64**, 65
Peter the Great of Russia, 17
Pineapple, 90, **91**
Poppy, **37**, 38
Post, Mae (Quinlan), **36**, 36
Post, Wiley, 36
Postage Stamp, **84**, 85
Potlatch, 11, **70**
Powell, Margaret, **20**, 22
Pratt Museum, **6**
Pribilof Islands, 19
Pugh, John Fraser, 30, 31

R

Rain Country Quilters, 6
Rainy Day Quilt Guild, 6
Ransberg, Miranda E., **97**, 97
Rasmuson, Elmer E., 7, 58, 59
Rasmuson, Jenny (Olson), **58**, 58, 59
Raven clan, **70**, 73
Red Cross, 66
Red Work, **37**, 37, **110**
Red and Green appliqué, **37**, **46**, **49**, **97**

Reed, Venetia (Fehr) Pugh, 30, 31, **64**, **105**
Ripinsky Rippers, 6
Rising Sun, **50**, 50, **51**, 51
Robbing Peter to Pay Paul, **105**
Roberts, Cora (Belt) or Amelia, **110**
Rocky Road to Kansas, **9**, **47**
Rogers, Will, 36
Rose, **62**, 62
Russian-American Company, 18

S

S.S. Princess Sophia, **31**, 31
Sailboats, **65**, 65
Sames, Anna Marie (Biehn), 47
Sanderson, Phoebe, 52, **53**
Schreinben, Lt., **18**
Scott, Valerie (Wilson), **30**, 30
Scroggs, Fannie Laura (Davidson), **38**, 38
Seal parties (*uqiquq*), 11, **75**, 75-79
Sears Company stores, 41
Seven Sisters, 94, **95**
Seward Quilters Group, 6
sewing kit, **29**
Sharp, Helena (Schaeffer) Smith,
    17, **27**, 27
Sherwood, Gladys "Happy", **68**, 68
Shissler, Pappy, **4**
Sitka Industrial Training School, 21, 73
Skagway, 28, 29
Skagway Museum, 6, 59
Smithsonian Institution National
    Museum of American History, 24, **25**, 25
Soldier's Quilt, 24, **25**, 25, 26
Sparling, Bertha Laura (Grossardt), **11**
Spence, Mabel Louise (Allen), **44**, 44
Spiderweb Star variation, **4**
St. Clair, Mary Rose (Bright), 86
steamship travel, 30
Steele, Maude (Kidd), **51**, 51
Steering Committee Members, 6, 13
Stickroth, George and Audrey, **110**
Stoltzfus, Lydia (Hartz), **81**, 82
Streak of Lightning, **93**
Strip, **69**
Summer and Winter pattern, **96**, 96

T

Tlingit quilts, 70-73
Triangle pieces and templates, **43**
Trip Around the World, **98**, 98
Tumbling Block, **41**, 41
Turnbull, Florence or Abigail, **4**

U

U.S. Army, 25
U.S. Map Quilt, **40**, 40
United States Army, 19
University of Alaska, 57

V

Valdez Museum, 6
van der Hoof, Gail, 9
Vancouver Barracks, 25
Vanderbilt, Lena, 23
Variable Star, **48**, 48

Varner, Frankie G., **112**
Ver Mehren, Hubert, **49**
Voris, Selma (Cross), **7**
Vriezelaar, Driekie (van Rootselaar), **42**, 43

W

Waldvogel, Merikay, **54**
Ware, Marge, 69
Waring, Frances (Charles), 29
Waring, Jeanette "Nettie", 29
Whig Rose and Carolina Lily, **46**, 46
Whitney Museum, 9
Widmark, Emma, 73
Wild Goose Chase, **8**
Willard, Caroline (Mrs. Eugene), 21
Williams, Mrs. Louis L., 23
Winans, Olive, **110**
Winter & Pond photographers, **17**, **70**, **72**
Woodman, Lyman, 25
Wrangell Museum, 6, **27**
Wyly, Minnie J., 62

Y

Yankee Puzzle, **102**
Yo-Yo, **39**, 39, **101**
Yukon Territory, 25-27
Yupik Eskimo, 74-79

Z

Zaldaris, Mary S., 37

JACK IN THE BEANSTALK, dated 1941, Frankie G. Varner, (1896-1964), Michigan; cotton, appliqué whole top, 38" x 56", Collection of Judy Reece, AQS 1145f. Judy's grandmother made this quilt for Judy's birth and signed it "Gram."